USING
POWER STANDARDS
TO BUILD AN ALIGNED
CURRICULUM

USING
POWER
STANDARDS
TO BUILD AN ALIGNED
CURRICULUM

A PROCESS
MANUAL

JOE CRAWFORD

CORWIN
A SAGE Company

CORWIN
A SAGE Company

FOR INFORMATION:

Corwin
A SAGE Company
2455 Teller Road
Thousand Oaks, California 91320
(800) 233-9936
Fax: (800) 417-2466
www.corwin.com

SAGE Ltd.
1 Oliver's Yard
55 City Road
London EC1Y 1SP
United Kingdom

SAGE India Pvt. Ltd.
B 1/I 1 Mohan Cooperative
Industrial Area
Mathura Road, New Delhi 110 044
India

SAGE Asia-Pacific Pte. Ltd.
33 Pekin Street #02-01
Far East Square
Singapore 048763

Acquisitions Editor: Arnis Burvikovs
Associate Editor: Desirée A. Bartlett
Editorial Assistant: Kim Greenberg
Production Editor: Veronica Stapleton
Copy Editor: Barbara Corrigan
Typesetter: C&M Digitals (P) Ltd.
Proofreader: Susan Schon
Indexer: Rick Hurd
Cover Designer: Scott Van Atta
Permissions Editor: Karen Ehrmann

Copyright © 2011 by Corwin

Printed in the United States of America

Library of Congress Cataloging-in-Publication Data

Crawford, Joe, 1946-

Using power standards to build an aligned curriculum : a process manual/Joe Crawford.

p. cm.
Includes bibliographical references and index.

ISBN 978-1-4129-9116-2 (pbk.)

1. Curriculum planning—Handbooks, manuals, etc.
2. Education—Curricula—Handbooks, manuals, etc.
I. Title.

LB2806.15.C6912 2011 375'.001—dc22 2010045949

This book is printed on acid-free paper

11 12 13 14 15 10 9 8 7 6 5 4 3 2 1

Contents

Foreword		ix
Dr. Jody L. Ware		
Preface		xv
Acknowledgments		xxi
About the Author		xxiii
Software Availability		xxv
1.	**Process Overview and Curriculum Issues**	**1**
	Chapter Expectations	1
	Process Overview	1
	What About National Standards?	4
	Survey of Current Environment	6
	What Are Power Standards?	16
	Process Summary	18
	Process Checklist	20
2.	**Designing the Work Process**	**21**
	Chapter Expectations	21
	Who Will Do the Work, and What Will They Do?	21
	Goals, Roles, and Responsibilities	26
	Process Summary	28
	Process Checklist	29
3.	**Developing and Deploying the Power Standards**	**31**
	Chapter Expectations	31
	Getting Started	31
	Developing Power Standards	37
	Deploying the Power Standards	42
	Publishing the Power Standards	44
	Gathering Feedback	45

Final Publication and Use of Power Standards   50
Process Summary   50
Process Checklist   51

4. The Next Step: Quarterly Instructional Objectives   53
Chapter Expectations   53
The Change Process Continues   53
Publishing and Communication Issues   54
Board of Education Action   57
The Group to Do the Work   57
What Are Quarterly Instructional Objectives?   58
A Curriculum System   60
Developing the Quarterly Instructional Objectives   61
Samples and Numbering the Quarterly Instructional Objectives 65
Realities of the Quarterly Instructional Objectives   69
Publishing and Reviewing the Quarterly
    Instructional Objectives   70
Process Summary   74
Process Checklist   75

5. Planning for Common, Aligned Assessments   77
Chapter Expectations   77
What Are Common, Aligned Assessments?   77
Why Use Common Assessments?   78
Stepping Out of the Box   81
Predesign Issues   82
Considering Assessment Options   85
Doing the Work   87
A Sample of Doing the Work   89
Further Applications of the Work   102
Publication and Storage Issues   105
Scoring and Using the Data   107
Final Thoughts and Use in Response to Intervention   109
Process Summary   111
Process Checklist   112

6. Special Concerns and Issues   115
Chapter Expectations   115
Overview   115
Common Curriculum and Formative Assessment Practices   116
Legal Mandates   119
Instructional Strategies and Methods   120
How Do We Begin?   123
Process Summary   124
Process Checklist   125

7.	**Troubleshooting and Follow-Through**	**127**
	Chapter Expectations	127
	Ready, Set, Go! The Feedback Loop	127
	Critical Questions	129
	Dealing With the Feedback	131
	Keeping the Project Alive	133
	Final Thoughts and Advice	137
	Process Summary	138
	Process Checklist	139

**Resource A: Standards-Based Curriculum
Guide Models and Related Documents** — **141**

**Resource B: Sample Power Standards and
Quarterly Instructional Objectives** — **149**

**Resource C: Suggested Forms for Developing Power
Standards, Instructional Objectives, and Feedback** — **157**

Resource D: Recommended Agency References — **169**

Resource E: Sample Results — **171**

References and Suggested Readings — **179**

Index — **181**

Foreword

There is significant focus throughout our country on improving public education. Federal programs from No Child Left Behind to Race to the Top are focusing on student achievement and college readiness to prepare our students for the twenty-first century global economy. It seems like everybody is talking about educational reform. Politicians claim to know what is in the best interest of educating our children and what the scorecard should look like for measuring success. Often it is the well-intended citizens who feel they have the right answer for improving the educational system. However, isn't it really the educational community who should be the experts and leading the charge in educational reform?

Joe Crawford is an educational veteran with experience as a classroom teacher, middle school principal, assistant superintendent of curriculum, and national presenter. Throughout the years, Joe has been successfully leading educators through the educational reform process with a focus on improved student achievement. This book is the how-to book for the educational community to lead the charge in educational reform with a focus on student achievement. As an educational leader, I have had the opportunity to implement the process of curriculum alignment, as described in this resourceful book, in many educational settings. I have implemented the curriculum alignment process at the elementary building level, in an elementary PreK–2 system, in a unit PreK–12 district, and presently in a large high school district. The process of curriculum alignment is doable when the steps described in Mr. Crawford's book are followed. I like to refer to the process as "a journey" when working with staff members engaged in the process. The journey process is a passage from one place to another. From my experience throughout the years, I do know that leadership matters and is critical for the process to be successful.

Why wouldn't an educational leader want to ensure that an aligned curriculum is in place in his or her district? Many studies have been conducted by educational leaders such as Mike Schmoker, Doug Reeves, and Robert Marzano. According to Marzano (2007), schools in the United States experiencing significant positive change in student performance have big-picture learning goals that align with the state, national, and/or college readiness standards; clearly defined and communicated student-friendly instructional objectives; and formative ongoing common assessment to measure student success in order to provide data for instructional adjustments in the student learning environment. Together, these components lead to a guaranteed and viable curriculum. Marzano further describes a guaranteed and viable curriculum as one that provides clear guidance to teachers, with the teachers discussing and agreeing to what content should be covered in each course, how it should be taught, and level of student mastery. The content must be articulated or taught well in the time available. This is important because curriculum coherence needs to exist. In the planning and design of the guaranteed and viable curriculum, educators need to agree that the big-picture learning goals (referred to as *Power Standards* in this book) and the instructional objectives are in logical sequence and vertical alignment with the entire instructional program. It is important to note that a guaranteed and viable curriculum is not scripted teaching. The learning goals and instructional objectives identify the "what" of teaching, not the "how." The how of a particular learning goal must be taught with considerable judgment or reflection on the part of the teachers (the art of teaching) within the parameters provided by the research on best practices (the science of teaching), with particular attention given to the learners' needs and style of learning or differentiation. Robert Marzano stresses that by implementing a guaranteed and viable curriculum, student achievement can increase by 16 to 41 percentage points. This is the reason educational leaders need to provide learning-centered leadership with deliberate efforts to align the curriculum, provide the resources for instructional materials, facilitate the purchase of the hardware/software for data warehousing, plan the professional development around the curriculum alignment process, and continue to focus on the shared vision of the school or district improving student achievement. Educational leaders need to ensure that there is a school culture focused on student learning and success. The district's vision needs to communicate student success, with everyone embracing his or her part in the accountability of learning.

The work of DuFour and Eaker (1998) speaks about the importance of a shared vision. A shared vision is a critical element of a high-performing school. Everyone from top leadership, including the governing board, to the student has to be part of the shared vision and believe in it. Shared vision motivates and energizes, creates a proactive orientation, and gives direction or goals along with roles and responsibilities to the staff in the organization. The shared vision establishes specific standards of excellence with a clear agenda for action. Mr. Crawford's book provides two models of a management tool known as Plan-on-a-Page. There are many benefits to utilizing this type of document beyond the fact that it eliminates binders full of strategic plans sitting on shelves in district offices to a one-page document. The brevity of this document is worth its weight in gold for the reason that it eases communication to all stakeholders, focuses on student achievement as well as many other measurable system goals, and makes it easy to manage the measures throughout the year and publicize performance. Shared vision begins with the governing board and this tool, Plan-on-a-Page. This tool is created by many stakeholders, including the governing board, administrators, and staff. It establishes a commitment by all to adhere to the plan. This tool allows for the governing board to stay focused on the goals/measures and lessens the intensity of individual agendas sidetracking the districts' initiatives. Governing board agendas for meetings can be built around the Plan-on-a-Page. Administrative evaluation plans can be designed with the goals and measures described on the Plan-on-a-Page. Individual schools, grade levels, subject departments, and students can develop their versions of the district's Plan-on-a-Page, aligning their goals and measures with the district's goals and measures. All in all, the district staff and community become the keepers of the vision.

As mentioned earlier, Joe Crawford's book, *Using Power Standards to Build an Aligned Curriculum: A Process Manual*, describes the importance of engaging the staff in the process of identifying the Power Standards and Quarterly Instructional Objectives as well as creating the common assessment for measuring student success. The process involves creating grade-level/department-level teams or professional learning communities. Power Standards and Quarterly Instructional Objectives are created by the professional learning communities using state, national, or college readiness standards along with their professional judgment. Rick and Becky DuFour advocate for what they call the team learning process (DuFour & DuFour, 2004). Although it can be challenging putting the process into practice, the process described in this book makes it quite straightforward and easy to understand. The professional learning teams need to clarify the essential common outcomes (Power Standards) per term or semester, by course or content; "unpack" or identify the Quarterly Instructional Objectives; and develop the common assessments with an agreed-on timeline for administering the assessments. Following the administration of assessments and collection of data, it is a critical component that the professional learning team analyze the results identifying and implementing improvement strategies. Rick DuFour states that the professional learning teams need to focus on learning rather than teaching, work collaboratively, and hold themselves accountable for results. The professional learning teams should focus on three questions:

1. What do we want each student to learn?

2. How will we know when each student has learned it?

3. How will we respond when a student experiences difficulty in learning?

In the process of curriculum alignment, progress monitoring by the professional learning team enables each teacher to determine how his or her students perform on every skill in comparison to all students who complete the assessment. This allows the team members to make decisions guided by data rather than by opinion. In the context of the team, teachers can provide the support needed to help each other address areas of concern. This process is described in this book as the Plan, Do, Check, Act model.

> *Plan.* Creating a curriculum through a development and alignment process including Power Standards, Quarterly Instructional Objectives, common assessments, and lesson plans with research-based instructional strategies
>
> *Do.* Implementing the lessons and common assessments
>
> *Check.* Reviewing the student data to evaluate student achievement, effectiveness of assessments, and focus of lessons
>
> *Act.* Revising the curriculum, assessment, and lessons according to student achievement data analysis

There is no reason to assess if there aren't going to be alterations, modifications, or adjustments made to address those students who haven't learned the skill to the level of mastery determined. This is known as progress monitoring. Intervention for students who are not successful is part of the formative assessment process and a factor that influences raising student achievement. An effective instructional strategy for raising student achievement is providing feedback to students on their progress toward the clearly defined learning goal or instructional objective. Students want teachers to understand what they have learned, take into account what they understood and misunderstood, and use this knowledge as a starting place to guide their continued learning.

This book presents many tools that can be used in the curriculum alignment process. Technology is a valuable tool for progress monitoring. Partners4results is an excellent software tool for maintaining the curriculum alignment process. This particular software is user friendly, is inexpensive, and provides educators with the information that they need to improve students' achievement. Assessments can be created that use multiple choices, are performance-based rubrics, or use extended response/short answer. The versatility of this software plays an important role in accurately measuring student learning.

As an educational leader, I believe that Doug Reeves states it best in his "blinding flash of the obvious." Our students learn what we teach them. If we never teach a concept to them, they will never learn it. If we assess them on what we have not taught them, whose fault is their failure? Curriculum alignment is the answer. As educators, we don't need legislation, state mandates, financially powerful individuals, and well-intended laypeople to create the "silver bullet" to address student achievement. Rather, we the educational community, experts both inside and outside our systems, need to lead the way and do what is right for our students.

On a personal note, I have worked with Joe Crawford for almost two decades. This book represents powerful ingredients for building an aligned curriculum and assessment system. This book is written in a format that clearly defines the steps and process that educational leaders can use to align curriculum in their districts. Joe has had a highly successful career as a principal and assistant superintendent of curriculum and experience working with the most knowledgeable educational researchers. Given this combination, this is a very useful book guiding educational leaders through the curriculum alignment and assessment journey. If implemented with fidelity, the process described in this book will take your classroom, grade level, department, school, or district from one place to another for student achievement.

—Dr. Jody L. Ware

Figure 0.1 Plan, Do, Check, Act

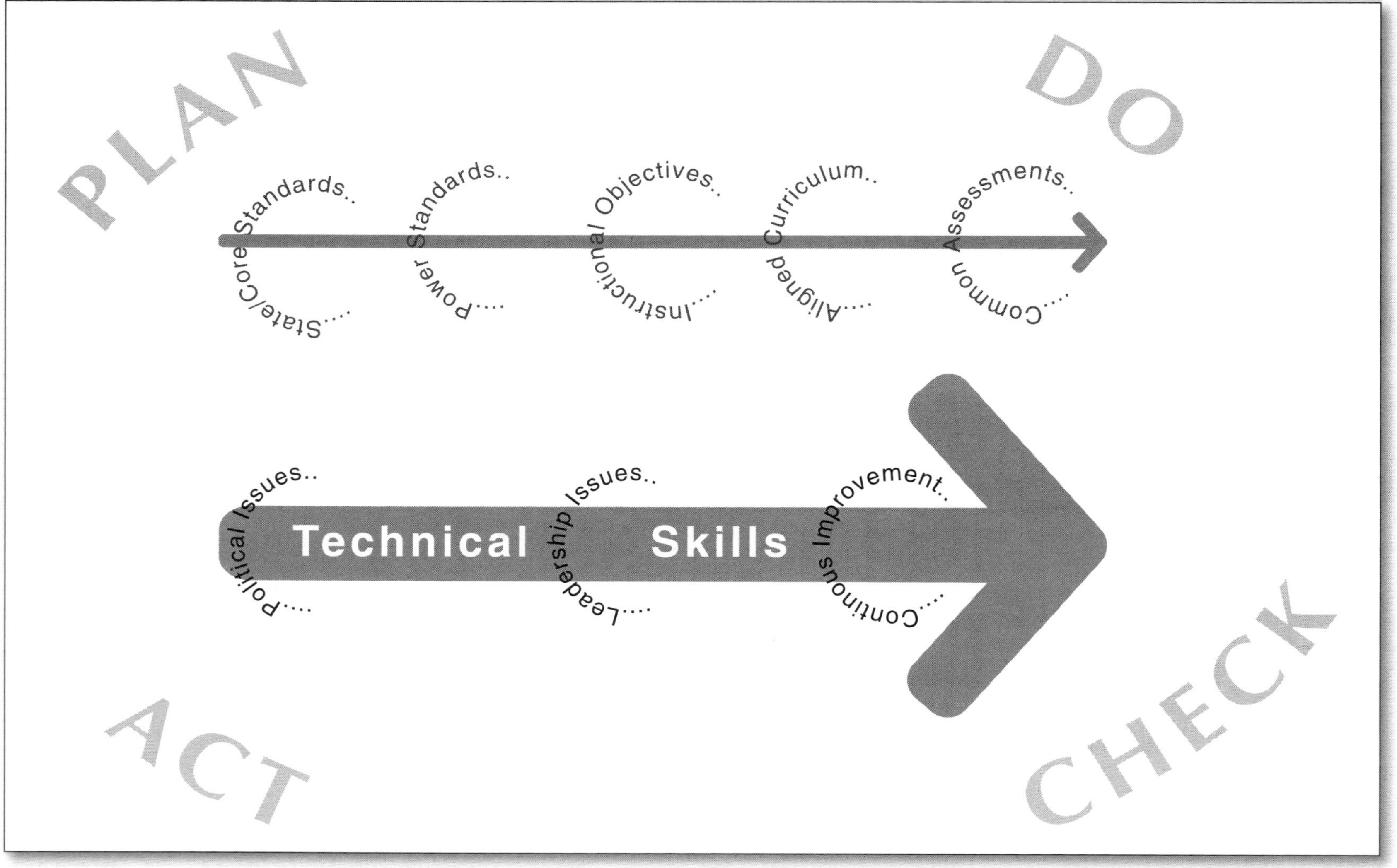

PLAN

DO

CHECK

ACT

Common Assessments....

....Aligned Curriculum....

Instructional Objectives....

....Power Standards....

State/Core Standards....

Technical Skills

....Continuous Improvement....

....Leadership Issues....

....Political Issues....

Preface

The journey from state standards to Power Standards to Quarterly Instructional Objectives to an aligned curriculum and common assessments appears rather simple in Figure 0.1 on the opposite page. However, as we all know, it is much more complicated than that. There are many additional steps involved in this process that must be deftly navigated if the journey is to be successful. This book is written specifically for you, the practitioner, who struggles daily with the many, complex tasks associated with public education while trying to improve student performance and do what is best for kids.

Power Standards have been around for years and are a process of looking at all the state standards in a particular state and determining which standards are so important and so central to the learning process that they must be learned by all students. This book will help you to involve the teaching staff in this important conversation, and in so doing, the teachers not only come to better understand the state standards but also come to agreement on exactly what it is all students must know and be able to do. This is a complex process and will be discussed in great detail in later chapters.

In addition to developing Power Standards, a concept that has been in use in public education for years, this book will explain the process of using those Power Standards to develop Quarterly Instructional Objectives, which will become the aligned curriculum so desperately needed by districts and schools to ensure student success. While totally based on the research and work of Doug Reeves, Larry Ainsworth, and others in the development of the Power Standards, these Quarterly Instructional Objectives are a new way to develop an aligned curriculum that is owned and understood by the local staff who developed that local curriculum and will add much to the communication process of helping students and parents understand the expected curriculum. These Power Standards and Quarterly Instructional Objectives will also be developed through a local process that takes the Power Standards for each grade level or content area and allows teachers to decide how to sequence instruction to ensure all students will learn the Power Standards. The Quarterly Instructional Objectives answer the question, If the Power Standard is the intended learning for the year, what must students learn first quarter, second quarter, and so on?

If I have seen farther than others, it is because I have stood on the shoulders of giants.

—Isaac Newton

These Quarterly Instructional Objectives are a different approach to the actual use of Power Standards, and they not only serve as the basis for the aligned curriculum but also are the perfect springboard for local educators to develop common quarterly assessments. If these five or ten Quarterly Instructional Objectives developed by the local professional staff represent the required learning for the first quarter, can those same local teachers develop assessments to measure those specific skills? Absolutely! These common assessments will then give classroom teachers the information they need about student learning and academic progress that will allow them to adjust instruction to improve student learning. These common assessments will allow teachers to work together to compare the results and the instructional strategies that produced those results. Additionally, these locally developed common assessments can be used as the progress monitors for the Response to Intervention process, thus allowing teachers to use assessments that measure what was actually taught and expected to be learned. We continue to work to create a system that bridges the link between instruction and assessments to help all children learn and teachers to use assessment measures that reflect their actual instruction.

This book is written to help practicing educators, central office administrators, building principals, instructional leaders, and classroom teachers, apply the work of the great masters, Doug Reeves, Larry Lezotte, Mike Schmoker, Rick Stiggins, and others. Additionally, the training and experience I have received in total quality management, and especially system reforms from Lynn Feaver, serve as the foundation for this entire work. I thank them for their help and guidance over the years. Additionally, I have infused this book with the lessons learned in working in complex educational systems that are struggling to survive and make a difference for kids. It is on their shoulders that I stand and hope this book will help practicing educators to successfully apply the ideas and research of the great masters in the real-world setting in which they work and live.

This book and its approach attempt to be as simple and straightforward as possible. Because the research is so crystal clear and well known, your time and this book's space will not be taken in recapping that research. An abundance of studies shows that these approaches work, but this book will not summarize or explore that research. I will refer to the research throughout the book; if the reader is looking for a research summary, this is not the book.

If you are reading this book, you must be serious about the change process. Know that the path to change is fraught with danger and land mines. We have all stepped on several of those land mines and been ambushed at the pass, yet we have lived to laugh about it. This practical advice, often contained in story boxes, will help you understand the practical aspect of the problems and help you avoid the land mines and the "stutter steps" that can cost time and commitment. Embarking on change is a journey you are freely choosing to undertake—enjoy the process and the people along the way.

> True Insanity—Doing what you have always done and expecting the results to be different.
>
> –Albert Einstein

Further, this book will look at the process of using the Power Standards to build an aligned curriculum and common assessments in more than just a linear progression of technical skills. The technical skills—the how-tos, if you will—will be addressed in a linear fashion, progressing from beginning to end in a step-by-step fashion. However, this book will also address the political and leadership issues as well as the continuous improvement mechanisms needed to make sure that these additional issues are addressed while the technical aspects of the change process are accomplished.

As you move from step to step in the logical progression of technical tasks needed to accomplish the creation of the Power Standards, Quarterly Instructional Objectives, and common assessments, the political, leadership, and continuous improvement issues will also be addressed. While these political, leadership, and continuous improvement issues will certainly be different at each stage of the linear development of the technical process, the book will also consider these issues and their changing demands and importance as part of the change process. As Larry Lezotte says, "It's simple, but it ain't easy."

It is imperative to change how the people interact within the system, and that is very difficult work. Changing the rules of engagement and the way "we have always done it" challenges beliefs that are deeply, though often unconsciously, held about the correct way to do things. True systemic change will transform daily interactions among members of the group, most important including what they talk about within that system. Conversations about students and learning and how to change what we, the adults, do to improve that learning must become part of the new system.

While many talk about radically restructuring American public education through continuous progress education, ungraded classrooms, longer school days, and longer school years, the financial and political realities of those solutions are beyond the sphere of influence or the realm of possibility for practicing teachers and administrators in America. The purpose of this book, and the advice contained therein, is designed to help you, the practicing teachers and administrators, do things here and now within the local building/district that can significantly affect student learning and forever change the educational system that so desperately needs changing.

Larry Lezotte and Kathleen McKee (2006), in their book *Stepping Up, Leading the Charge to Improve Our Schools,* explain that the leader will need two things to change the current system:

1. knowledge, skills, and behaviors required to lead change, and

2. a proven model of organizational change that is relevant to education.

Both of these observations are true, and this book will focus on both the "proven model of organizational change that is relevant to education" (the technical knowledge strand) and the "knowledge, skills, and behaviors required to lead change" (the political, leadership, and continuous improvement strands). This book will frame the work of Reeves, Lezotte, Schmoker, Stiggins, and others within the total quality management framework of continuous improvement with a generous portion of leadership and political advice based on forty years of experience.

Furthermore, the work advocated in this book is absolutely possible in the real-world environment of public education. Doug Reeves with his 90-90-90 schools (90 percent minority, 90 percent poverty, and 90 percent meeting or exceeding state standards) and Larry Lezotte with his litany of effective schools (schools that show a huge improvement in student learning despite challenging demographics) present irrefutable proof that this work can be done. This work is done by ordinary people, but these ordinary people dare to do things differently. The successful people follow generally the same change formula—the agenda of the effective schools movement, the data-driven decision-making model, the continuous improvement model as outlined in total quality management, or some combination of these approaches.

USING THIS BOOK

The Sample Results section shows real results obtained by schools and districts that have followed the work outlined in this book. These are results for students on various state assessments. The data paint a picture of results obtained by following the national research in typical school districts. These positive results were produced by school districts and buildings functioning in the real world, with all of the problems and issues you deal with on a regular basis in your own situation. The people in these buildings and districts chose to do things differently to produce different results, improved results for the students they serve. You have the same choice to do things differently and follow the national research to improve student performance; this book will help you do just that.

Each of the chapters closes with a Process Summary section. This is an attempt to summarize the critical points contained in the process so you may refer to a quick set of points to help in understanding the entire process. The Process Checklist gives you the opportunity to go through the checklist as a kind of quick review to make sure you have done or considered all the important tasks.

Actual forms used by the author in applying this work are included in the book and are set in boxes to separate them from the regular text of the book. Spacing has been reduced for ease of publishing.

Public education is fraught with local politics as well as volatile social issues beyond the control of education. The purpose of this book is to help you negotiate this difficult terrain without getting blown up in the minefield that is called the change process. As the title says, this book will help you use the concept of Power Standards, a proven national model, to build an aligned curriculum and assessment system that will improve student learning. This use of Power Standards as the basis for an aligned curriculum and common assessments and the specific, commonsense ways to accomplish these tasks using local people are what set this book apart from the others. May it help you along in your always challenging and difficult, but incredibly important, journey.

While Figure 0.1 (page xiv) may suggest a linear system, it is not the author's intent to present this as a totally linear process. There is definitely a sequence to the work, but it is a scaffolding process wherein one thing builds on another. The Plan, Do, Check, Act model that surrounds the graphic is there to remind the reader that this entire process is built on continuous improvement and a cycle that constantly examines and improves our work.

To ensure that I am a good consumer of my own product and put this work through its own continuous improvement loop, I would ask every reader who sees something that could be expanded on, could be improved, or leaves the reader unsure of the intended action to please contact me at jtcrawford@comcast.net to share your concerns or ideas for future publications or revisions. If the experiences and ideas can be shared in future editions, it will help all of us be more successful.

Acknowledgments

Once I begin to say thank you, as I am supposed to do in an acknowledgment, I find it very hard to stop saying thank you—there are so many people who have helped me in my journey I couldn't possibly mention them all. I am told to limit my thanks to the people who have helped with this book and the processes in this book, so here is my best effort to say thank you without boring the reader, too much.

In looking at any work on curriculum alignment and systemic reform, the work and inspiration of Larry Lezotte, Doug Reeves, Mike Schmoker, and Rick Stiggins has to be acknowledged—they are the pioneers, the keepers of the vision, and the giants on whose shoulders I try to stand.

Thanks, of course, to the schools and districts that have trusted in me enough to try this approach to improving student performance—their faith and support as well as participation helped us all grow, I hope.

Thanks to Lynn Feaver, the consummate total quality management/ Baldrige expert and helper and thinker and doer on systems—he taught me all about how to do this work and what it all means. The Plan-on-a-Page is his inspiration, and his guidance in doing this work is priceless.

Thanks to the editor, Arnis Burvikovs, for his support and hard work in getting my best work out of me. I look forward to doing this again.

Thanks to those who participated in this book by helping with clarifications and moral support in this effort—Karen Sanders for her advice on the special education issues, Heidi Downing for her help with the assessment work, Deb Lischwe for her early editing help, Sue Valkema for her formatting and listening, and Jon Dingler for serving as my sounding board for ideas.

I must, once again, thank my family, especially Kat, Ben, and Sara, for all of the help and support over the years as "Daddy's working (again or still, depending on your perspective)" was the answer to many requests to do things. I hope my work didn't take too much away from your lives, and thanks for bearing with me—I love you all very, very much, more than words can say.

PUBLISHER'S ACKNOWLEDGMENTS

Corwin gratefully acknowledges the following individuals for their guidance and editorial insight:

Lisa Graham
Program Specialist, Curriculum
    and Staff Development,
    Special Education
Vallejo City Unified School
    District
Vallejo, CA

Odalys Igneri
Curriculum Specialist
Chief Achievement Office
Students With Disabilities and
    English Language Learners
New York City Department of
    Education
New York City, NY

Julie Kopp
Curriculum Coach
Penfield Central Schools
Penfield, NY

Elizabeth J. Lolli
Superintendent
Monroe Local Schools
Monroe, OH

Darla Miner
Reading Consultant
Orange Public Schools
Race Brook School
Orange, CT

Diana Peer
Master Principal Leader
Arkansas Leadership
    Academy
Fayetteville, AR

Sharon M. Redfern
Principal
Highland Park Elementary
    School
Lewistown, MT

Deborah Wahlstrom
President
Successline Inc.
Suffolk, VA

Jody L. Ware
Superintendent
Mundelein Consolidated High
    School District 120
Mundelein, IL

Jill M. Zitnay
Reading Consultant
Turkey Hill School
Orange, CT

About the Author

 **Joe Crawford** spent thirty-six years in public education at the high school, junior high, middle school, and district level as an English teacher, assistant principal, principal, and assistant superintendent focusing on improving student performance. He has been recognized by the Illinois State Board of Education in the Those Who Excel program and by the Carnegie Foundation with the National Systemic Change Award. Additionally, he was the principal of a twice-recognized National Blue Ribbon School of Excellence and met two U.S. presidents as part of that recognition. He was also chosen by the Illinois State Board of Education and the Milken Family Foundation as a National Distinguished Educator. He has also been active in total quality management and continuous improvement, and his work reflects the tenets of these industry-standard approaches to improvement. While he was doing this work, his district received a Silver Award from the Baldrige Foundation.

Following the work of Larry Lezotte, Doug Reeves, Mike Schmoker, and others, he works with local districts to apply this invaluable work and research in the real world of public schools and kids—making the transition from research to reality possible and even pleasant. He works with teachers and districts to build capacity and to create a common sense of mission through shared ownership of solutions. By involving those who will implement decisions in the actual decision-making process, he helps create a sense of buy-in and a much deeper understanding of state standards and the improvement process, leading to sustainable, long-term improvement in student performance.

Software Availability

In doing work as complex and demanding as this, it is almost impossible to do so without using electronic technology to store, score, analyze, and warehouse all this information. There are several software packages out there that readers may be using and/or considering to do this work. It was very difficult to write this book without referencing the software that is being used to address this process specifically, and I did the best I could; however, it is, in my judgment, imperative to share this software and its capabilities with the reader so the reader may better understand the power and potential of this process.

Throughout this book, in the discussion of the processes and forms, there is reference to the Partners4results software package that can be used to do this work. To ensure a level playing field and to better demonstrate these processes, the reader is encouraged to go to the following URL: www.partners4results.org/demo. When prompted, please complete the sign-in process. Once you sign in, you will be able to navigate the website for a complete product demonstration.

This website has video to show you how to navigate the site appropriately. This will give you firsthand experience using this software and the Internet to construct Power Standards and Quarterly Instructional Objectives and the electronic format for doing so. You will also be able to see the curriculum-mapping component, the publishing capabilities, and the assessment alignment capabilities of the software, giving you a first-hand experience with the software discussed in the book. There are also help icons and e-mail capabilities available on this site to answer any questions you may have.

I hope this helps you better understand this work and this process without being blatantly commercial about it; I could think of no other way to share this with the reader. I just read Patrick Lencioni's *Getting Naked,* and he had these same concerns with his work and his company. He turned his book into a fable and "changed the names to protect the innocent," but my writing skills precluded that approach; I hope my more direct approach offends nobody.

This book is dedicated to my family, especially Kat, Ben, and Sara, and my friends and fellow educators, especially those in Crete-Monee, Freeport, Morrison, Mundelein, and Ship Rock, who have helped make me who I am. What I have accomplished has been possible through their guidance, hard work, and support. A special thanks to Dr. Jody Ware, who is incredible and whose help and support have been critical to my growth and the growth of this process.

1

Process Overview and Curriculum Issues

CHAPTER EXPECTATIONS

This chapter will give an overview of the entire process of using state standards to develop Power Standards, Quarterly Instructional Objectives, and common, aligned assessments. The chapter outlines the process of developing the curriculum documents that the local staff creates, understands, supports, and is able to implement. The first step in the change process is to determine where the organization is so the issue of existing curriculum realities within which the work must be done are dealt with and suggestions are shared for understanding and using the local politics to help advance the project. Those readers whose curriculum is currently guaranteed and viable may wish to skip the sections in this chapter about curriculum issues.

PROCESS OVERVIEW

This book will describe the process shown in Figure 0.1 (page xiv), that is, how the local practitioner can work with his or her own local personnel to use the state standards as the basis for Power Standards, as developed and operationalized by Larry Ainsworth and Doug Reeves. The book will explain how, once these Power Standards are developed by a task force of local educators, to take the Power Standards in a completely different direction than is normally taken and use the Power Standards as the basis for an aligned curriculum and common assessments.

Through a process involving a task force of the same local personnel who developed the Power Standards, work will next be done to develop Quarterly Instructional Objectives. These Quarterly Instructional Objectives answer the question, If the Power Standard is the expected student learning for the year, then what must students learn first quarter? Second quarter? Third quarter? Fourth quarter? These Quarterly Instructional Objectives are developed through the same professional process as were the Power Standards. That is, local teachers, using the Power Standards (which are based on the state standards), will decide what specific skills must be learned and in what order those skills must be learned to ensure all students move toward mastery of the Power Standards in a logical progression of skills built on previously acquired skills.

These Quarterly Instructional Objectives will be aligned to the Power Standards and the subskills used by the state assessment to measure the content area. For example, if your state uses algebraic reasoning, number sense, integers, geometric reasoning, and statistics and probability to define math, then steps will be taken by the design task force to ensure all of these subskills are taught throughout the year in a predetermined sequence as determined by the local professional educators. Unlike pacing guides or lesson plans used by some schools or districts, these locally developed Quarterly Instructional Objectives will be anywhere from five to ten specific skills that will be taught by every teacher in that grade level or subject area during the academic quarter designated by those professionals. Please note that there is no attempt to determine *how* these things will be taught—that is the art of the individual teacher—but the task force will decide on and agree to *what* specific skills will be taught and *when* these skills will be taught throughout the school year.

These Quarterly Instructional Objectives can then serve as the basis for the development of common assessments, again by the same local personnel who have done the curriculum alignment work described above. While developing such common formative assessments has always proved a huge, almost insurmountable problem for most local educators, the use of the Quarterly Instructional Objectives and the very specific skills they identify as the sole basis for the instruction and the assessments for the specific quarter greatly reduce the complexity and consternation of the assessment development process. With such specific directives as "The student will add, subtract, multiply, and divide integers" (a real Quarterly Instructional Objective developed by one of my partner schools), the development of the common assessments, as well as the development of simple quizzes and tests, can be done and shared by local teachers within the grade level or course. Since this process ensures all teachers are teaching the same skills in approximately the same order, such sharing between teachers is now possible.

Through the numbering system used (this will be shared in Chapter 4, Samples and Numbering the Quarterly Instructional Objectives section), these Quarterly Instructional Objectives can then be used to develop common assessments to measure student progress toward achieving the Power Standards and to develop real-time data showing student performance on specific skills. By tagging common assessment items to specific Quarterly Instructional Objectives, teachers can get instant feedback about which students have mastered which Quarterly Instructional Objective and which students have not, thus allowing for tutorial work that is focused on a specific, diagnosed weakness rather than the student's having failed the test. Specific areas of strength and weakness will be identified, and teachers will be given real-time data to drive decision making within the instructional process.

During this common assessment development process, it's important to remember what not only total quality management but also Wiggins and McTighe (1998) tell us about beginning with the end in mind and backwards design. As these Power Standards and Quarterly Instructional Objectives are developed, we must be aware that they will become the basis not only of all instruction but also of our common assessment system; therefore, we must consider their assessment potential as they are written. Can we write assessment items to measure these intended learnings? We will discuss this in more depth in the chapters that follow, but the reader is reminded of its importance to the process.

The last step in this process is developing a system to use all of this data to improve instruction and learning. We must begin to use these formative assessments and to generate leading indicators of student performance that will affect student performance. The creation of this kind of system to use all of the student performance data will take time and commitment, perhaps years, but it is a critical part of the process to ensure that we use these new formative assessments to alter instruction to improve student performance.

This process can be made much easier through the use of the Internet-based software package provided by Partners4results (www.partners 4results.org). This software package was developed as a result of the work the software company did with the author and is now available for those who wish to use software and the Internet to enable the process to be completed much easier and more efficiently. This process will be part of the descriptors used throughout the book, and the reader may use and explore this software package online at www.partners4results.org/demo.

Further, all of this curriculum alignment and development work will be done in a continuous improvement environment with built-in checks and balances to ensure the process and the product are continually improved. Steeped in total quality management practices and especially the Plan, Do, Check, Act cycle, this book will give the reader the opportunity to walk through the process in a step-by-step order to implement the technical changes needed in this process while continuously addressing the political and leadership realities and continuous improvement issues inherent in the change process. Each of these steps will be explained in the appropriate chapters in far greater detail, but an overview of the entire process is important to help the reader understand the expected learning.

The Plan, Do, Check, Act cycle is frequently amended in education by replacing the Check part of the cycle with Reflect; that is, we take the time to reflect on the impact of the work we do and the best ways to improve that work. Some even add Reflect as an additional step in the process. Any of those derivations can be applied and will work, so long as the point is that we are looking at our work and correcting and amending that work based on results that the work is producing or failing to produce.

> During my early days as a district administrator, we were discussing the Plan, Do, Check, Act cycle; the task force was discussing how we in education have become the masters of the Plan, Do cycle. No matter what the problem or social issue, we can write a curriculum for it or develop a program to address the need. We are constantly in a state of developing curriculum or programs to address problems— a kind of constant Plan, Do, Plan, Do . . . cycle without ever checking to see if the new programs work (affect the desired behavior). While we were all laughing and enjoying the moment, one of the teachers interjected, "No, Joe, you plan, we do," the point being that we need to make deliberate efforts to see (Check or Reflect) if the programs we design and deploy have any impact on the intended behaviors.

WHAT ABOUT NATIONAL STANDARDS?

With all the excitement and trepidation surrounding the imminent adoption of national standards, many people are asking if districts should just wait for the new national standards to be implemented and then move forward with curriculum alignment projects. Why do all the work of aligning to state standards if those state standards are to be replaced by national standards? That is an important question and deserves some time and space in this book and in the reader's thinking.

America really is serious about adopting and implementing the new national standards, and that is a really good thing. We, as a country, need to define what it is we want all of our children to know and be able to do to meet the challenges of the twenty-first century and beyond. To remain competitive at the international level, we must produce world-class learners with world-class skills, and the move to national standards can be a great step in that direction. Once these world-class standards are adopted nationally, we can then begin to have the conversation about changing the structure of public education to meet those world-class standards.

The first thing we must remember is what Larry Lezotte teaches in his public speaking: there are only two kinds of schools, improving and declining. As institutions, we are either improving our services to kids and the results we produce, or we are declining. There simply is no way to hold our own, tread water, or whatever words may describe attempts to maintain the current state of education in this country. That being said, how do we justify inaction or a holding pattern until the new national standards are adopted and implemented?

Will we say to today's learners that there is a new initiative coming, and when that new initiative hits, we will respond to it and improve services then? That is hardly possible, nor is it the reason we became educators. We became educators because we want to help prepare the future leaders of the world, and that means all of our children all of the time. We simply cannot wait for the next innovation, the next big thing, the next whatever. We must operate within our current reality and do the absolute best we can do with the technologies and issues we currently have.

This is an opportunity for districts to be proactive in the face of the coming national standards. It will take time to finalize these national standards, but that time frame is not the issue. There are several issues that mandate curriculum alignment despite the impending national standards, or perhaps because of them:

- This curriculum alignment process will take the staff through the development of local Power Standards and instructional objectives and increase the staff's knowledge of and familiarity with standards in general.
- This series of curriculum alignment activities will prepare the staff to better understand and deal with standards-based education issues.
- This curriculum alignment work will lay the groundwork for a curriculum and assessment system to make the eventual transfer to national standards and the many issues that accompany this new initiative.
- The district will not be starting from scratch when it comes time to implement national standards but rather will have a framework and a process in place and functioning to deal with this new initiative.
- The district will be way ahead of the curve where research tells us we need to be.
- Can the district afford to do nothing with the standards initiative but wait until the change is made and then react to that change? Even a year can be a long time to delay such important work. Can the district afford to sit by and tell the community it is waiting for the new national standards to improve services? Can the system afford such inaction?

- The national standards, while they will not be completely aligned with any state's standards, will have lots of commonality with many existing state standards. Particular skills may move from one grade level to another, and subskills within the content area may be defined somewhat differently by the national standards, but the basic skill set will be transferable from the state to the national standards. That simply has to happen to allow a transition from state to national standards.

This is a chance for proactive districts and people to get ahead of the curve and position their districts much better than other districts that fail to see the opportunity in this new national standards initiative. The opportunity to be a leader in this transition process is here, but only for districts that choose to be leaders.

SURVEY OF CURRENT ENVIRONMENT

As discussed earlier, those districts that have already done this curriculum alignment work may choose to skip this section. But for the rest of us, as we prepare to do this work, it is important to do what total quality management calls an environmental scan, that is, to assess the curriculum system currently in place. Once we know where we are, it is easier to chart where we want to go. Before we begin the journey, let's look to see where we are.

Some systems do a SWOT analysis as described in total quality management, that is, an analysis of strengths, weaknesses (internal), opportunities, and threats (external). These four areas are shared with a leadership group, and each person is asked to respond to each area privately—what do they personally see in each area? Following time to do such individual work, the individual tables or small groups are asked to come to consensus on the group's answer to the questions posed. The facilitator then does the same exercise with the entire group to come to consensus on the issues.

The advantage of this approach is that it builds group consensus on problems and issues. However, it is time consuming, and it is not always possible to involve all members of the organization in this process. The main issue you will want to come to grips with is the current state of the curriculum process in the district since this is the area of focus for this project. Frequently found in many districts are the curriculum realities discussed in the next couple of sections. It is important that readers understand these curriculum issues so that they may make sure these curriculum issues are addressed through this process of curriculum alignment.

There are districts that have done exemplary work in this curriculum alignment process, and they are to be congratulated for their efforts. It is, however, still critical to ask these questions to make sure these issues are considered by everyone doing this work. If your district has done this work, that is great. If not, you will find a blueprint for doing the work in this book. So let's examine the critical questions.

Do You Even Have a Curriculum?

While at first glance this may seem like a silly question, it is indeed a very important question to be asked. As Mike Schmoker, Larry Lezotte, Doug Reeves, and others tell us, although a guaranteed and viable curriculum is the first and most important step in improving student performance, not all districts have such a document. A curriculum is guaranteed when the local education system can guarantee it is taught in every classroom in the district. A curriculum is viable when it is aligned to the state standards and assessments.

Many people who are not involved in education assume that the curriculum in schools and districts is controlled by a very tight set of expectations and academic skills that are universally taught at specific grade levels and times of the year. Many also believe that these curriculum expectations are held across school, district, and even state lines. In many, if not most, systems, nothing could be further from the truth. Every district in this country has been free to determine what will be taught and when it will be taught. This freedom, combined with the natural evolution of organizations, has led to a national educational system that is all over the board about what is taught and when it is taught.

For several years in the 1990s, I taught graduate-level curriculum courses to teachers and administrators at a couple of colleges and universities in the south suburbs of Chicago. These teachers and administrators practiced in some very prestigious suburban districts as well as some of the more challenging environments. During the first class meeting of every semester, I would make the same offer—if anyone in the class could bring the district curriculum documents that drove his or her instruction and determined what he or she taught, that student would receive an A on the first test. No such grade was ever given.

People could sometimes find curriculum documents through a friendly secretary or older teacher who just happened to know where one of the old curriculum guides had been stashed. Usually written years ago, as a personal favor to the teacher or administrator, these documents were generally found on a forgotten shelf somewhere. Documents that were yellow with age (and even a few still published in purple spirit-masters, for those old enough to remember that technology) or dusty and forgotten in some storage cabinet were occasionally produced, but nobody ever produced a current document that really drove instruction. Following such a revelation, we discussed what, then, does determine what the teachers teach the kids. It boiled down to the same answers—the textbook, what the teacher liked, what the other teachers recommended, and so forth. In such an environment, how can we expect real curriculum alignment to happen?

While state standards attempt to standardize curriculum expectations across a single state, there is still much discretion at the local level in deciding what will be taught and when it will be taught. In fact, even mentioning state standards as a kind of state curriculum can elicit cries of anguish about academic freedom from many practitioners. Over the years, the public education system has been built through local control and independent decision making, and in many cases, classroom preferences have determined what is taught and when it is taught.

Real curriculum documents that drive everyday instruction in a meaningful way simply do not exist in many districts. What really gets taught is frequently a matter of choice or chance, not design. But do not blame the teachers for some kind of plot to avoid responsibility or academic content. Teachers, for the most part, are hard-working, child-centered, dedicated professionals who are doing their best to survive in an environment rich in accountability and poor in support. The educators discussed in the story box have simply never been told exactly what it is they are expected to teach.

> When I first taught high school English in a large, prestigious, suburban high school, I was given a 400-page curriculum document containing about every skill known to man, which I was expected to teach to my sophomore English students. When I asked for more specific direction, I was told to "figure it out." I made those instructional decisions for my students, and the other sophomore English teachers (I believe there were six) made their own individual choices.
>
> While most teachers strive to do the best that they can in such an unaligned system, there is no possibility that the efforts of that entire English department, or any other academic department or grade level in the country, can be even remotely aligned to any outside document such as state standards or the ACT, or anything else for that matter. And how did the sophomore English teachers' efforts serve the needs of the junior English teachers? Not at all, I'm sure. However, since all teachers were pretty much free to do as they saw fit, it never really mattered. In an unaligned system such as this and many others in America, teachers simply taught what they thought to be important or what they enjoyed and let the test scores (if there were any back then) fall where they may. Besides, what drove the education system for many years was the bell curve, which told us that some kids were supposed to achieve, and some kids weren't—"Don't blame me, I just taught 'em."

Remember, as Larry Lezotte tells us, we are not in trouble because we did something wrong; we're in trouble because our mission changed. We went from compulsory attendance to compulsory learning for all students, but we have not changed our system to reflect our new mission.

What about the state standards that almost all states have since adopted? Don't those clearly outline the learning expectations for all students? No, because many states have done little to operationalize standards across the entire state in a focused, understandable way. While some state standards have been around a long time, the standards themselves have received scattered and often minimal attention. Also, simply putting the standards on the state's website with some explanatory directions and links to other sites does not operationalize state standards nor reform the existing system into a standards-based system.

> While working in the middle school environment years ago, I presented a program about creating middle schools from junior highs at a state conference and explained to the audience that the conversion from a traditional junior high to a fully functioning middle school was a three- to five-year process with staff development, research, and so forth required to really do the work.
>
> Following my presentation, a school board member approached me and explained how wrong my timeline was and how his district had made the conversion in a single board meeting by passing a resolution changing the name of all four junior highs to middle schools. It was quick and efficient and had worked, or so he thought.

Also, let's not blame the administrators for a lack of dedication or leadership. Again, the administrators I have dealt with, for the most part, are hard-working, dedicated people. Some feel overwhelmed, to be sure, but they are a great resource and partner in this curriculum leadership initiative. Administrators provide the leadership, and they must absolutely be a part of this initiative. However, few national models for effectively aligning curriculum documents to the state standards exist, and these are hard to find and daunting to many administrators who lack experience in curriculum and instruction. Since each state has its own standards, a national model is hard to create, but this book will explain such a model that can and has worked. More professional educators need to become aware of these proven approaches through conferences and books like this, which give local people the kind of support and advice they need to move the change-agenda initiative forward.

> In a discussion with a social studies department that was looking at the state standards for a particular grade level, the entire department saw that the standards for that grade level were evenly divided between the American Revolution and Westward Expansion. One agitated teacher said to me, "Joe, you don't get it. I became a social studies teacher because I love to teach the American Revolution. Are you saying I can't teach the American Revolution?" Before I could answer, one of the other teachers in the department said, "Yes, you can still teach the American Revolution, but you just can't teach it all year long like you have been." That is the point. We have a very good, well-intentioned teacher spending all his time and passion on a favorite topic and ignoring the other parts of the state standards.

First and foremost, the most important curriculum question that must be asked is similar to the question I asked those graduate students years ago: Can anyone produce the district curriculum documents that drive instruction and determine what kids learn? Does the district have a single document that guides instruction in every classroom in the district? Not just the elementary classes, not just the academic classes, not just the regular education classes, but all classes—from kindergarten through high school in all content areas. Has the district formally decided and published, and the board adopted, a single document or series of documents that describe what every child must know and be able to do?

So back to the original question posed above—Can anyone produce the district curriculum documents that drive instruction and determine what kids are expected to learn? Does the district have a single document that guides instruction in every classroom in the district? Once a system produces that document, if it exists, the reader can go on to the next steps, ensuring that the document is truly aligned to the state standards and assessments, that it is universally deployed, and that those using it are fully prepared to do so. But we first have to find that curriculum document or admit it does not exist. Either answer is a good answer in the change process—once we know where we are, plotting where we are going is easier.

Remember, if you can't find the curriculum guide or teachers don't know whether it even exists, the district really doesn't have such a document. Finding one through a secretary who has been around for years and knows where the document is hidden or stored does not count. The curriculum guide must be a real, living document that teachers use to design instruction and follow faithfully to determine what all kids must know and be able to do.

In a district that I recently worked with for two years, I posed this same question about the existence of a curriculum. The curriculum person with whom I was working was quick to confirm that they indeed had a district curriculum document, which even had a pacing component to it that told teachers what to teach and when to teach it. I was impressed and asked to see it.

A year and a half later, we were still looking for it. Several people had heard of it, some even claimed to have seen it, but nobody could produce the document itself. After two years, we agreed that they might have such a document, but nobody could find it.

Do You Have Three Curricula?

Currently, in many school districts, there are three distinct and separate curricula, as shown in Figure 1.1. The first curriculum (Curriculum) is the curriculum that is published by the district. This is the existing written document, if there is one, which outlines the expected learnings for every student in every class. The second curriculum (Instruction) is the curriculum taught

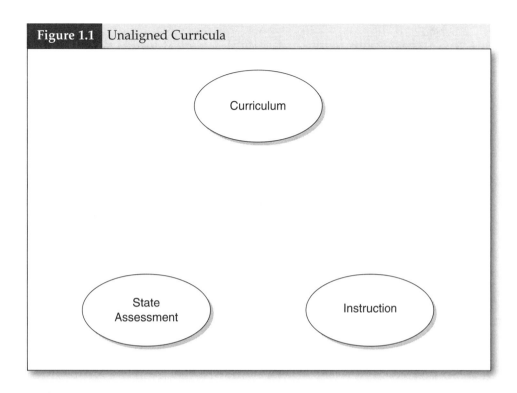

Figure 1.1 Unaligned Curricula

by the teachers, which may or may not be consistent throughout the district. In many districts, the second curriculum is not the same as the district curriculum and, in fact, varies from classroom to classroom within the same grade level and within the same school—basically teachers are making individual decisions about what is and what is not taught. The third curriculum (State Assessment) is the curriculum that is assessed by the state assessment. Please note the absolute lack of connection among the three curricula—that is the real problem in many current student performance issues—there is no alignment among these three curricula, especially between the curriculum being taught to the students and the curriculum being assessed by the state.

While talking to a high school science department comprising four teachers teaching the introductory biology class, we got into a discussion about the most critical parts of biology. The first teacher was quick to say that understanding cell structure is the most important part of learning biology. Teacher 2 disagreed and explained that understanding the chemical reactions within the cell is critical to understanding biology. The third teacher corrected both of the others and explained why knowing genetics is most essential. I cannot even remember what the fourth teacher selected as the critical factor in understanding biology, but I believe my point is made. Can anyone even remotely believe that a coordinated, aligned curriculum in biology exists in that building? Better yet, can the teachers who teach the follow-up course, Chemistry I, get a group of students who are equally prepared for the next course in the mandated sequence?

Curriculum alignment will help not only the current classroom teacher but also the classroom teacher who will have those students in the next course or grade level. I have since had conversations similar to that presented in the story box with many science and other subject-area teachers, with similar results.

Larry Ainsworth, who coined the term *Power Standards* and did the work that led to those Power Standards, talks about asking teachers, Who has taught all the state standards assigned to their grade level? Of course, nobody has, so the questions follow, How did you choose? Based on what? The problem is, of course, that all teachers use different criteria and choose different standards, resulting in the biology issues discussed above. That leads to the current state of affairs in curriculum—there are very few coherent, well-defined, and aligned curricula that are taught by entire school systems, much less used by entire states.

Figure 1.2, based on the work and writings of Lisa Carter (2007) and others, shows the ideal state of curriculum alignment. Please note that in the diagram, there is no intent to establish the state assessment as the only thing taught. That would be foolish. The point is to ensure that the state assessment is central to what our children are taught—educators owe students that if they are expected to demonstrate proficiency or better on that state assessment.

In addition to the skills and standards contained in the state assessment, the curriculum that is taught covers many issues and topics, which is as it should be, but we need to take steps to ensure the state standards and assessment system are central to our instructional focus.

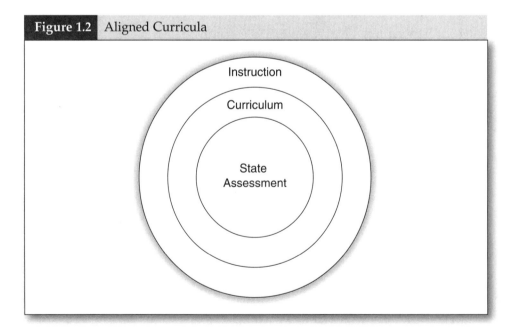

Figure 1.2   Aligned Curricula

Instruction

Curriculum

State
Assessment

Due to the secretive nature of the state assessments and the difficulty of finding and using released items, teachers do not always know specifically what students are expected to do on the state assessments. Think about that! Public education has well-intentioned, hard-working professionals preparing students for assessments that the teachers themselves have not seen and do not really understand. Would America tolerate such a system in medical school? Commercial pilot school?

That is my point, exactly. If the district does not exercise its management prerogative to decide, publish, and ensure what gets taught and when it gets taught, the lack of focus and agreement on curriculum is a fait accompli. It is also critical to point out that while I call for districts to exercise their management prerogative to decide, publish, and ensure the curriculum that is taught, I do so in an inclusive, teacher-driven process that involves those who will implement the decision. Curriculum decisions, that is, aligning to the state standards, must be subject to the judgment of those closest to the ground, the teachers who do the daily work. While the process must happen under the guidance and supervision of the administrative team, the decisions must ultimately be made by the teachers who will teach the skills. It is a collective work that must engage all. The teacher voice must be heard and be a major component of the decision-making process.

> In my work as a consultant, it is not at all unusual to be in junior high and high school classrooms and witness English teachers teaching parts of speech and subject-verb agreement, even though that is a second-, third-, or even fourth-grade state standard. Seeing rote drill in times tables or work with fractions in junior high is also not unusual. These teachers are not trying to hold back kids to keep them from being successful. They are doing what they think is right, but the system has failed both the kids and their teachers by not clearly defining and enforcing a guaranteed and viable curriculum.

One of the forms we use to help districts assess their current curriculum realities is presented in the What the Research Tells Us box. Teachers are asked to respond to this survey, building principals then collate the responses for their buildings (instructional leaders need to know the current curriculum reality in their buildings), and then the person responsible for curriculum at the central office collates the results for the entire district. As with many of the forms shown in this book, the spacing has been changed to make publishing easier.

WHAT THE RESEARCH TELLS US

The research and work of Larry Lezotte, Mike Schmoker, Doug Reeves, Rick Stiggins, and many others continually point out the importance of a guaranteed and viable curriculum in improving student performance. The research is crystal clear on the impact of an aligned and viable curriculum as the first step in improving student performance, and gains of 25 to 30 percent are seen by doing this work.

That being said, let's talk about where you and your building/district are in that process of creating a guaranteed (taught in every classroom in the district) and viable (aligned to state standards) curriculum. Please respond to each of the questions below as a kind of reality check on your current efforts and progress toward a guaranteed and viable curriculum.

On a scale of 1 to 5, please rate your current status in each area listed below the scale.

Scale

1 = Not really a strong area—we've talked some about it but that's about it.

2 = We have looked at this issue and have discussed what we should do but have not begun any of the work.

3 = We are in the planning stages but have not really selected our approach or set a budget, timeline, and so forth.

4 = We have begun the process, have a game plan in place, and are moving forward on a timetable.

5 = We have accomplished this goal; our current state reflects national best practice, and we could share our work with others.

1. Our school/district has an actual, published curriculum document in place that is aligned to the state standards and state assessment system and is readily accessible for all.	1	2	3	4	5
2. Our school/district has an actual, published curriculum document that defines and drives all instruction in the school/district and is used by all professional staff to plan instruction.	1	2	3	4	5
3. Our school/district has spent the time and the resources to ensure all of our professional staff understand the state standards and are able to use those standards as the basis for designing instruction.	1	2	3	4	5
4. Our school/district has spent the time and the resources to ensure all of our professional staff understand the state assessment system, the skills all of our students must demonstrate, and how they must demonstrate those skills.	1	2	3	4	5

5. Our school/district has a set of common, aligned formative assessments that are used by all professional staff on predetermined dates to measure student progress toward achieving state standards.	1	2	3	4	5
6. Our school/district is able to provide real-time data to our staff to report the results of the common, formative assessments in a timely manner so said results can be used in the reteaching loop to address specific, diagnosed weaknesses.	1	2	3	4	5
7. Our school/district has the electronic capability to report to students and parents that same real-time data about student performance on all of our common, aligned assessments.	1	2	3	4	5
8. Our school/district has the electronic capability to enable our administrators to monitor curriculum and instruction and to create and share data charts about current instructional practices with staff for the purpose of improving student performance.	1	2	3	4	5
9. Our school/district has an electronic curriculum map that is interactive and available 24-7 for our staff to share their successes and challenges in curriculum implementation.	1	2	3	4	5
10. Our school's/district's curriculum and instruction system formally uses continuous feedback (Plan, Do, Check, Act) to ensure the curriculum is constantly being improved, refined, and made more effective.	1	2	3	4	5

This preassessment is designed to help you see and understand the current state of your school's/district's curriculum and instruction system so that you may better prepare to move forward and improve student performance. In a perfect world, you would be able to rate each area a 5, but that is seldom the current reality.

The critical issue with the form in the What the Research Tells Us box is determining whether there is a central curriculum document that defines and drives all instruction—not a document somewhere on a shelf or server that nobody uses or responds to but a real, living curriculum document. This process will help you move toward this kind of document.

> While I was working with a district on developing math Power Standards and instructional objectives, we were having our vertical articulation discussion to make sure we had covered all the essential skills and in the correct order. The fifth-grade teachers began the conversation with, "When we get the new fifth graders, they can never divide fractions." The fourth-grade teachers quickly responded, "Don't blame us, they teach that in third grade." The third-grade teachers responded with a blank stare and replied, "We thought that was part of the fourth-grade curriculum." The point is obvious; without serious, ongoing discussions like the ones required in the creation and maintenance of Power Standards and instructional objectives, such errors are happening everywhere.

WHAT ARE POWER STANDARDS?

The concept of Power Standards was introduced by Larry Ainsworth (2003a) in his book *Power Standards* and refined and operationalized by Doug Reeves during years of groundbreaking work and research. If the state standards are truly to be the basis for all instruction in the state, then educators must decide which standards at each grade level are the most critical to be taught. Since teachers cannot possibly teach all the state standards, let's decide on the state standards that students absolutely must learn and then do everything to ensure students learn these identified standards.

In current writing and research, there are several similar terms that essentially define Power Standards. They are referred to as "understandings" (Wiggins & McTighe, 2007, cited in Westerberg, 2009, pp. 33–34), "measurement topics" (Marzano, 2006, cited in Westerberg, 2009, pp. 33–34), "essential learnings" (NASSP, 2004, cited in Westerberg, 2009, pp. 33–34), and "Power Standards" (Reeves, 2001, cited in Westerberg, 2009, pp. 33–34). What all of these terms are essentially defining are those essential skills that all children must know and be able to do.

That is the long and the short of Power Standards. A group of professional educators must sit down in an organized fashion with certain documents and decide which of the many state standards are so important and so critical that they must be learned by all students.

So how will your system decide which of the state standards will be used to determine the Power Standards? While the complete list of state standards can be overwhelming, further work and cooperation among the teaching staff can refine these long lists down to the most important, most critical skills, which will then become the basis of all classroom instruction. These are the Power Standards that guide classroom instruction and assessment and provide the kind of laser-like focus the teacher needs to deliver quality education for all students. A more complete discussion of this process is in Chapter 4.

In his book *"Unwrapping" the Standards*, Larry Ainsworth (2003b) proposes the following exercise to help teachers understand the standards. After selecting the standard to be "unwrapped," the group carefully reads it and underlines the key concepts the student is expected to learn (important nouns and noun phrases); the group then identifies and circles the verbs (what the student is expected to do with that concept—identify, evaluate, analyze, and so forth. The concepts are what students must know and skills, while performance verbs are what they must be able to do with what they know. This gives the entire group a graphic representation of precisely what the state standard is expecting the students to know and be able to do to meet the standard.

I have worked with John Antonetti, a prominent national consultant in educational reform, and he does something very similar but even more striking. He has the group use two highlighters, one color for important nouns and the other color for verbs. This shows in a visual way the skills and performances being required in the state standards.

Either method works and helps teachers come to a greater understanding of the state standards. The group then goes on to put the information into a graphic organizer, which can be as simple as putting concepts (nouns) at the top (things they need to know), skills in the middle (what they need to be able to do with the concepts), and topics/context (what content we will use to teach the standard) at the bottom.

Let's make one thing completely clear; the Power Standards are not proposed in any way to oppose state standards. State standards begin to clarify and codify what educators want students to know and be able to do, but these long lists of state standards do not provide teachers the kind of clarity needed to guide instruction. As explained throughout this book, the alignment of the three curricula is critical to improving student performance, the most important goal. What the system must do is provide the time, structure, and leadership to come to consensus on the most important and most critical learnings for that system. Once the system decides to work together to do this, a process must be developed to ensure those learnings are universally taught and assessed in a systematic way. Deployment issues will be explored in detail later.

> I often relate the standards, assessment system, and many of the complex issues facing educators to the shape and size of a football. If only the football were round and a bit smaller, say like a soccer ball, it would bounce much straighter, take fewer "weird" hops, be easier to catch and throw, and generally make life easier for the players. However, the nature of the game is designed around this unusually shaped ball and its many idiosyncrasies. You can't change it, and if you did, it would destroy the uniqueness of the game. Learn to live with it, deal with it, and enjoy it, and do your best.

Also, it must be understood that this exercise of identifying Power Standards is not designed to, nor should it venture to, argue about whether the state has selected the appropriate state standards. The state standards are what they are, and the local group cannot change them, so do not spend time arguing about whether those standards are what they should be, whether the state followed a good process in determining them, and on and on. All of that is irrelevant. The state standards are here to stay, and it looks as if they will be replaced with national standards. If any of these standards are modified, they will be modified by a group other than the local one working with this process. Don't waste energy discussing that which cannot be changed, and get on with the task at hand, using the state standards to focus instruction and learning in the building or district.

Once the information about the standards is gathered and feelings are expressed, then the system must integrate this information, data, and judgment into a singular Power Standard, an expression of the most critical, most important skills that all students must know and be able to do in a grade level or course.

> Once these essential learnings are identified, we must do what Doug Reeves discusses in *Making Standards Work* (2003): "Pull the Weeds Before Planting the Flowers" (Chapter 13) and take a long, hard look at letting go of those classroom activities that do not help us teach those essential learnings (pp. 103–105).

As discussed in numerous places in this book and throughout the curriculum world, the current curriculum is "a mile wide and an inch deep." Power Standards give educators the opportunity to correct that once and for all. This process allows educators to make a conscious, deliberate decision about what all students must know and be able to do and limit that to a teachable, learnable number of skills.

PROCESS SUMMARY

The actual process has not yet begun, so you are studying and preparing to do the work. Make sure you have done your homework and are totally familiar with Power Standards, Quarterly Instructional Objectives, and common assessments. Also, take the time to really understand the internal politics and the current curriculum system and how it has functioned in the past. Remember, the purpose of this project is to move forward, not prosecute the past.

Political Issues

Understanding the local politics is also of paramount importance in this stage of the process. To bring a system to consensus on an issue as important and complex as defining the real curriculum, that is, to define the curriculum that is actually taught and assessed, is a huge undertaking, and bringing all members of the system on board, supportive of this initiative, is demanding work. That work demands not only an understanding of the technical issue of Power Standards but also an understanding of and willingness to work within the political realities of the local system.

Leadership Issues

Use your knowledge of the political system and your professional leadership skills to listen to people, to help them understand the project, to create buy-in, and to answer questions and clear up concerns. Your commitment and dedication to helping all participants understand what you are doing, why you are doing it, and their role in that change is critical to moving this forward. Take your time and do it right.

Continuous Improvement Issues

Continuous improvement skills are not required at this stage of the process, other than constantly referring to the Plan, Do, Check, Act cycle as a part of the finished product. Remember, you will not be asking people to commit to a single answer that will remain in place forever; you will be working with them to create curriculum documents that will be examined and refined on an annual basis. Whatever decisions are made, the Plan, Do, Check, Act cycle will be used to continuously improve the work and process.

Technical Skills

At this stage of the process, you must make sure you totally understand the concept of Power Standards, how to develop them, and the importance of doing so. If more information is needed in understanding or developing Power Standards, further reading of this book will be helpful, but it is imperative you feel comfortable with the concept of Power Standards and the need for them before you move this initiative forward.

PROCESS CHECKLIST

Make sure you do or consider the following:

☐ Educate all members of the educational community about what Power Standards are and the process to be followed in developing those Power Standards.

☐ Develop and deploy a specific plan to share the work and thinking of the task force.

☐ Ensure, as the leader, that your knowledge of Power Standards and the entire process is complete. If needed, an outside consultant can be brought in, or you may choose to do this work yourself.

☐ Take the needed steps to understand the local politics and to bring as many people as possible on board for the project. Future problems may be avoided by particular attention to these issues early in the process.

☐ Deal with and address the political issues identified in the district as you design the work, addressed in the next chapter.

☐ Do the work to assess and understand the current state of curriculum in the district. This may entail use of the survey included in this chapter, or you may judge that it is not needed.

2

Designing the
Work Process

CHAPTER EXPECTATIONS

In reading this chapter, you can expect an overview of the technical steps involved in designing the work process as well as an explanation of issues to address as you design that work process. There will be an explanation of the technical steps involved in establishing and organizing the task force and assigning the specific tasks to be accomplished by that task force. This will be followed by the political and leadership issues involved as well as the steps to ensure that a continuous improvement cycle is part of the work from the beginning.

WHO WILL DO THE WORK, AND WHAT WILL THEY DO?

Now that you have done the work outlined in Chapter 1 and understand the concepts of Power Standards, Quarterly Instructional Objectives, and common assessments, it is time to identify the group that will actually do the work. This work involves the technical steps of designing and seating a task force and the work involved in giving them their charge as well as the inservice and staff development to help them move the project forward successfully. A budget, of course, must also be established and shared with everyone early in this process.

Additionally, it is imperative to build a sense of group purpose and commitment among the group doing the work. Members must feel empowered and motivated to do this work because it is what is best for kids and will improve student learning and the entire professional atmosphere. We will create what Rick Dufour calls a professional learning community, and we will work together to make a positive change for our students. Educators became educators because they want to work with kids and make a difference. This important work is the perfect opportunity to help them heed this higher calling and make a difference. There is much work by Dufour and others on the professional learning community and how to help build such an environment while doing this work.

Group Membership

It is time to decide who will do the work and what, exactly, they will do. The group who will actually do the curriculum alignment work must be representative of the larger organization. If this is a districtwide task force, as it should be in a process as important as determining the district's Power Standards, and the district is large enough to warrant such a selected, representative task force, then leadership must make sure that the task force represents a diverse cross section of the district. The size of the district will largely determine this selection process. In relatively small districts, I have worked with the entire faculty in designing Power Standards.

> Imagine what would happen to the Ford Motor Company if its management allowed itself to think, "This year we've built the ultimate in automobiles. Further improvement is impossible. Therefore, all experimental engineering and designing activities are hereby permanently terminated." Even the mammoth Ford Motor Company would shrivel fast with this attitude.
>
> —David Schwartz
> (see www.haphits.com/improvement/successful-improvement/)

Further, make sure membership on this task force does not conflict with other current district initiatives. If a functioning subject area task force is already working on a particular curriculum issue, that task force must be made aware of and/or included on this new Power Standards task force so nobody feels undermined. Depending on the district's current curriculum setup, there may be groups already assigned tasks around curriculum or grade level areas that could be seen to be in conflict with the new task force. If there is a standing English Curriculum Committee, what is its role in this new Power Standards initiative? Is there a district Reading Council? Is there a district Math Task Force?

Make sure to consider these existing groups and make special efforts to draw them into the new process, or at least make sure they are aware of the new direction and their role in that new direction. People serving on existing curriculum groups are frequently informal leaders within the organization, so alienating them can be particularly damaging to new efforts. Nothing alienates people quicker than feeling their current work is being undermined by a new group.

What about involving administrators in this new work? Are they part of this work? Absolutely! Each grade level or department task force should have an administrative presence. The administrator helps to make sure the task force is organized, meets timelines, gets paid, has refreshments, and so forth and also attends to "administrivia" (time sheets, sign-in forms, stipends). The lion's share of the actual work of the first-grade task force is done by the first-grade teachers, who are the experts in first-grade learning, but an administrative presence will help the group get things done on time, arrange meetings, get refreshments, get paid, and so forth.

When I was an assistant superintendent for curriculum and instruction and struggling with the transition to a standards-based curriculum, I became embroiled in the soon-to-be-infamous Butterfly Unit. For years, and I mean *years*, the third grade had done a butterfly unit in the spring that amounted to students' designing, painting, and building sets of butterfly wings, culminating in the parade of the butterflies—a walk around the inside of the building with the entire community invited to watch. Parents videotaped this incredibly cute parade of bright-eyed third graders dressed as butterflies, while grandparents who remembered when their own children had butterfly wings now saw their grandchildren in the butterfly regalia—it was a happening.

Spring was also the time of state testing in this state, and third grade is one of the tested grades. As the thrust on student performance and accountability swirled about, I asked *the* question—So which state standards does this two-week butterfly unit meet? Wow! What kind of heartless so and so was I? How could I object to something so adorable? The kids (and their parents and grandparents) loved it, much more than they loved me. But, hey, somebody has to ask the tough questions. While the crisis resolved itself and the unit was redesigned around specific state standards, it is an important question to be asked of any unit— Which state standards are being taught?

I am not opposed to a butterfly unit or any other interdisciplinary unit, but the unit must relate to the state standards. With twenty-four years of experience at the middle school level, I support interdisciplinary instruction as long as the unifying factor of any instructional unit is a state standard or several state standards that become the building blocks for activities that help kids internalize and more fully accomplish those state standards.

In smaller districts, it may not be possible to have an administrator on every grade-level task force or to have a task force for every grade level, but an administrative presence should be helpful to facilitate the group's work. If building administrators are to be the instructional leaders that research says they must be to drive the reform initiative, then these administrators must be present and participate in the curriculum process—gone are the days when the building principal could say, "I'm too busy running the building to get involved in curriculum projects." The system cannot expect teachers to believe this initiative, or any other initiative, is a priority to the leadership of the school if the building leaders excuse themselves every time the work begins.

This is not to say the principal must lead every facet and activity, but principals must be involved and active, showing by their presence, participation, and interest that they see this as a top priority. As professionals seek to identify the key skills students will be expected to learn, the principal's presence adds stature and sometimes conciliatory help so that everyone sees the work as important and meaningful.

Depending on the district's level of expertise and/or the expertise of the local Educational Service Center or State Department of Education, the local district, with such regional support, may be able to lead this project. If nobody is available locally, outside consultants can be brought in to help relatively inexpensively. Normally, the Power Standards development phase can be begun and assignments of the work by local personnel can be completed in two days of consulting. A follow-up consulting day may be necessary, based on district size and resources, to review the work and coordinate the work product. The important issue is that the consultant build local expertise and not do all the technical work. The consultant should have specific, technical knowledge necessary to the project that local personnel do not have, but it is imperative that the project build local expertise so the work may continue after the consultant leaves.

While the consultant may be important to lead the group's work, someone from the district must "own" this project—the Project Owner. That absolutely must be someone with decision-making authority who is committed to the project's success and reports to the superintendent or board. A consultant may have lots of knowledge about a subject, but he or she has no authority or control over district personnel. Meetings must be called, subs arranged, payment agreed to, food provided, publishing responsibilities met, and so on. If someone from the district is not committed to the project's successful completion, the consultant cannot make it happen. While bringing in an outside consultant to help in the developmental phase of the process may be justified, it is essential to recognize that the consultant's role is to build local competence. As Confucius says, "teach a man to fish"; so also in the educational environment, outside help should be used to build local expertise, enabling local educators to continue and expand the effort on their own.

I worked with a struggling district that hired me to create Power Standards and Quarterly Instructional Objectives. This all sounded great, but the administrator assigned to work with me was not involved in the decision to bring me in, nor was he ever really told his own goals, roles, and responsibilities. He saw this entire project as just one more thing he had to do in an already overbooked schedule, and frankly, he resented my alleged authority in the project. He felt I had total responsibility and was put out when I needed him to call meetings, arrange payments, run copies, or any of the things that require a local presence and authority.

While the project produced some impressive results, the rift between that administrator and me based on the failure of the local district to identify our respective roles in the project was insurmountable. I do not blame that local administrator who was victimized by a system failure. Because our goals, responsibilities, and expectations were not clarified, the project went away after a successful first year with lots of local teacher support.

Group Organization

Leadership will want to divide the group into grade-level teams for grades that are self-contained and into departmental groups for grade levels that are departmentalized. While the entire group will be together for the initial presentation explaining Power Standards and outlining the group's goals, roles, and responsibilities, much of the real work of the task force will be done in grade-level or departmental settings. This entire group can be quite large, but leadership should limit individual grade-level groups or departmental groups (those groups actually doing the grade-level/course curriculum work) to three to five people. In some departments, particularly within the high school, the entire department may want to do the actual work of identifying the Power Standards for specific courses, and a representative of that department may serve on the district-level task force. This works well, but leadership must be careful not to create large, unwieldy groups. This will depend on the size of the district, the time of the year, and the ability to get staff involved.

Always select a representative group that will have lots of credibility with the rest of the staff. It is important that you consider both formal (positional) leaders and informal (influential) leaders in the membership of groups. This task force, like all leadership groups, cannot be all male, all white, all black, all experienced teachers, or all anything else. Diversity does not happen by accident or by election; it must be deliberately designed into the group, and it is the responsibility of the Project Owner to make sure diversity in membership happens.

Also, this curriculum alignment work must be done by local people. Leadership cannot simply bring in an outside auditor to check the curriculum for alignment and move on from there—local educators must do this work to ensure local people have the expertise needed so they truly understand the state standards and alignment issues. By giving local people the support to make this alignment happen, leaders ensure that local people have the ability to continue this initiative and effectively deploy the new curriculum documents once the curriculum development process is completed.

Production Issues

Prior to beginning this curriculum alignment work, leadership should arrange for the production of packets of state and local curriculum and assessment materials to be used by the task force. Those packets should include the state standards, any local curriculum materials, state assessment frameworks, and any other appropriate materials. These will vary from state to state, based on which documents are available. This work is generally facilitated by the Project Owner.

As leaders prepare the packets of state standards for committee members, most teachers will not find the complete set of K–12 state-published standards to be of much help—they want to know what specifically they are to be held accountable for in their particular grade levels or courses. Leaders, then, need to present the state curriculum materials in that format, either by grade level or department. It is most useful to download the state standards and separate them into grade-level or department-level bundles. That means, for example, preparing a single document containing the kindergarten standards for all academic content for the kindergarten teachers, then doing the same for the first-grade teachers, second-grade teachers, and so on. At the high school level, such materials are prepared and bundled by subject area or coursework, again depending on what is available from the state. A complete set of state standards may be available.

When the local district gets to the point in the school experience where the organizational structure is built around departments (fifth grade, seventh grade, ninth grade, whatever), then publish the standards accordingly. For example, publish all the math standards for the building configuration, such as seventh- and eighth-grade math standards, together, doing the same for the other subject areas/departments in the building. This will result in grade-level and/or department sets for the secondary schools. The methodology used in the process will promote sharing across grade levels, but all teachers tend to want to have the standards for their own particular grade levels or departments.

GOALS, ROLES, AND RESPONSIBILITIES

Now that leaders have identified the group, decided the organizational issues, and dealt with material production issues, the group must be given its marching orders, that is, its goals, roles, and responsibilities.

In total quality management, it is a given that most groups fail because they do not understand their goals, roles, and responsibilities. Therefore, all members and groups must understand these three dimensions of their work from the outset. When setting up task forces, some authors even recommend formal job descriptions for these groups and their members. In my experience, it is sufficient to establish the goals, roles, and responsibilities in a group setting with input from all to ensure consensus.

This requires preplanning, but the Project Owner must know in advance the expected outcomes of the group's work, the givens, and the nonnegotiables. That is to say, if there is a specific expectation of a course sequence, the anticipated elimination of some other program, or any other predetermined goal of the group, everyone needs to know that before beginning the work or even accepting the assignment as a member of the task force. Let's look more specifically at what this means.

Goals

What are the goals of the group? What specific work are we to do? Are we to rewrite the entire K–12 curriculum? Is there a specific format required for publishing? Can different grade levels develop different formats? Can different departments develop different formats? Are there deadlines and specific publishing expectations? Come to consensus on these and any other important issues, and make sure to share this information with everyone.

Roles

What is my role as a member of this group? Participation is a given, but make sure to share that expectation anyway. Will members be expected to do research? Will their work need to be submitted in a specific format? Will that format be electronic? What about communication? Will members be expected to share the group's progress and issues with their constituencies? Will members be expected to bring their constituency's concerns back to the group? Is confidentiality a piece of this? Discuss these issues, and come up with a set of agreements. What is the budget for this project, and how may it be spent?

Responsibilities

What are my responsibilities? Do I have to report out on a regular basis? To whom? Does this group report out to another group? Who has final decision-making authority? Am I responsible for "selling" the contents of this document to any other group? To the board? Make sure everyone knows the expectations.

In one district I worked with, these goals, roles, and responsibilities as well as the entire curriculum development process were made part of board policy. This clarified and legitimatized the entire process and its direction. Moving curriculum work to this level of importance sends a powerful message to everyone in the educational community about its importance and expected processes.

An honest discussion not only will clarify these issues for task force members but will help increase the likelihood of the group's success. Commit these agreements to writing, and share them with the members of the specific work group and the entire district. This will eliminate many of the common complaints about group membership and responsibilities.

These goals, roles, and responsibilities must be generally decided on as the group begins to work together, but the group may discuss these goals, roles, and responsibilities and make minor changes if needed. Again, the Plan, Do, Check, Act cycle is used to ensure continuous improvement. The person(s) chosen to lead this work must be aware of and receptive to these goals, roles, and responsibilities and comfortable enough with them to discuss and finalize them.

It is now time to begin the work. You have done your design work, so it is time to move forward. Schedule the first meeting of the task force, and begin the work. This work will be clearly defined in the coming chapters.

PROCESS SUMMARY

This part of the process deals primarily with the steps the Project Owner must take in establishing the task force structure to do the actual work, organizing and seating the task force, and making sure the task force understands its exact responsibilities and parameters.

Political Issues

Your political skills will be particularly important in the selection of the group to do the work. Creating a diverse, representative group of people and bringing them on board committed to the project will require skills on the Project Owner's part.

Leadership Issues

During this stage of the project, the leader must ensure appropriate group involvement, selection of the right people to do the work, and a transparent process understood by all.

Continuous Improvement Issues

The work of the group has not really begun, but people must constantly be reminded of the tenets of total quality management—decisions based on data, involvement of those implementing the decision in making the decision, and decisions based on customer needs—and the use of the Plan, Do, Check, Act cycle throughout the project. Make sure these things are reflected in the design of the task force and its work.

Technical Skills

At this stage, you are designing the process for completion of the work, so you have to make sure you have identified the right group to do the work; have given them their goals, roles, and responsibilities; and have assigned a budget that is sufficient to complete the task. The entire district must also be aware of the process and its goals, roles, and responsibilities.

PROCESS CHECKLIST

Make sure you do or consider the following:

☐ Communicate, communicate, communicate to make sure everyone in the district is informed about the work and its goals.

☐ Create the task force to do the work, and ensure that it is diverse and representative of the entire district.

☐ Establish a budget that is sufficient to complete the work—remember to consider task force meeting expenses; stipends for any additional work, if needed; and food costs for meetings, if needed.

☐ Make sure the new task force does not conflict with or undermine existing groups.

☐ Make sure all members of the task force thoroughly understand Power Standards.

☐ Ensure an administrative presence throughout the project.

☐ Establish a publication and distribution process—who will be responsible and what process will be followed.

☐ Make sure the task force has all of the materials needed for its meetings—paper, computers, Internet connections, projection systems, and so forth.

(Continued)

(Continued)

☐ Clearly define the administrative role as supportive, with the task force making the curriculum decisions.

☐ Consider help from outside resources—the State Board of Education, the Regional Office of Education, an outside consultant, and so forth.

☐ Prepare state standards and assessment documents in grade-level and department formats for distribution to the task force.

☐ Ensure that existing district curriculum documents are published and available for use by the task force.

☐ Establish the task force work group structure—grade-level teams, departmental teams, and so forth.

☐ Assign goals, roles, and responsibilities, and discuss those with the task force to ensure understanding.

☐ Clearly establish communication expectations to ensure this is a transparent process—all issues may be shared between the task force and the rest of the district.

☐ Design a communication process to share the work of the task force.

3

Developing and Deploying the Power Standards

CHAPTER EXPECTATIONS

This chapter will go through a step-by-step process to create Power Standards from your own state standards and/or common core standards. The chapter outlines the process to use in creating a curriculum document that the staff understands, supports, and is able to implement. The chapter delineates the exact technical steps to take as well as the pitfalls and problems to consider before and during the journey to Power Standards. The chapter then goes on to outline the process of deploying those Power Standards, building in the continuous improvement cycle and mandating their use in planning instruction.

GETTING STARTED

Now that you have done all the design work, organized your task force, and made sure all the needed professional development is in place, it is time to begin the actual process of writing Power Standards, using your own local people. The process begins with the first task force meeting. As a reminder, you have made sure the task force is representative of the entire educational community and their tasks are clearly defined prior to this first meeting.

However, as a fail-safe, it is time to go over the goals, roles, and responsibilities of the group, making sure everyone understands these and is willing to move forward. Also, some groups feel a need for rules of engagement, the rules that will guide the discussion during the process; these are readily available from multiple sources, or the group can develop its own.

Remember, this entire process is about a collaborative approach and people working together to accomplish something for the greater good of all; feel free to use some group-building activities or fun warm-ups to bring the group members together and help them feel good about the work they are going to do. The middle school literature and the work of Rick Dufour and others can be valuable resources here, as can the local guidance counselors who enjoy building this group cohesion and sense of purpose. This work is about a collaboration to do the right things for our students, not another task No Child Left Behind has foisted on us.

The Project Owner should also make sure all appropriate state standard, common core standard, and state assessment documents are available and in an appropriate format. These state standard documents should be organized by grade level and subject in the self-contained, elementary school structure of the district. That is, the first-grade teacher representative should receive a packet with all of the first-grade state standards, assessment documents, and existing curriculum materials. The same should be true for every grade level. Once the school organizational pattern moves into departmental or team structures, the packets should be assembled to meet those needs. All junior high math teachers should get all of the math materials mentioned above; the same goes for English teachers; and so forth.

Materials for the group doing reading will also be distributed based on the organizational pattern of the school/district. If reading is taught by a content specialist, then a representative of that group should get that packet. If the reading Power Standards are to be developed by some other representatives—classroom teachers, for example—then plan accordingly. Remember, once the Power Standards are developed, they will be shared with all teachers in the building, and this can truly help every teacher in the building support reading instruction.

An important point to understand here is that the Power Standards, Quarterly Instructional Objectives, and common assessments will be developed by those people who use them on a regular basis. Third-grade work will be completed by third-grade teachers, with help as needed. Wood shop teachers, if the decision is made that noncore departments will do this work, will work only on wood shop curriculum materials. Social studies teachers will see the curriculum work from other areas so they can support that work when it is appropriate, but they will have no responsibility for doing that work. One of the critical issues of total quality management is that work product is created by those who will do that work, so we will make sure those people doing the work are designing the work.

The exact documents available from particular state educational agencies will vary markedly from state to state. Each state has different documents available, from released assessment items, to preparation materials, to delta standards, to assessment frameworks, to blueprints, and everything in between. Make sure the Project Owner has done his or her homework and has all the appropriate state standards and state assessment materials available. In addition to the state educational agency, many states have regional educational facilities to help with this process. A friend at one of these agencies can prove invaluable as you search for all the materials that will help. Additionally, networking with someone from a neighboring district who has done some of this work can be very helpful. It is imperative, however, that the most appropriate documents are available to the task force at or before the first meeting.

Once these materials are distributed to the task force, take the time to go through them in great detail to make sure everyone at the table understands exactly what they mean. These documents, especially some of the assessment documents, can be very complex and need to be understood by all participants if they are going to significantly contribute to the process. Since each grade level or department has a similar set of documents, it is relatively easy to work through the documents to make sure everyone understands them.

Below is the actual worksheet I use in this phase of the process. It is an attempt to bring all participants to the same place in their understanding of the documents they have and how they will use those documents. Feel free to amend it or use it as you see fit. As with other forms, spaces have been deleted for ease of publishing.

POWER STANDARDS DOCUMENT SEARCH

1. Which state standard and/or common core standard documents do you have, and approximately how many state standards are you expected to teach?
2. In these documents, does the state give any directions for refining the standards or limiting the number to a more teachable group of standards?
3. In the state assessment documents, how many content areas are assessed, and which subskills or strands are measured within the content area (i.e., math—number sense, algebraic reasoning, etc.; reading—vocabulary, inferencing, etc.)?
4. In the state assessment documents, which subskills or strands are tested and to what percentage of the test (i.e., math—number sense: 24 percent, algebraic reasoning: 26 percent, etc.; language arts—word origin: 24 percent, vocabulary: 18 percent, etc.)?
5. Are there sample items or released items available in these state documents or in other state documents? If so, where, and how do we gain access to those items?
6. What other documents, if any, does the group feel it needs to do a better job with this assignment?

This discussion guide will bring all participants to the same place in their understanding of the documents that they have and will be using and give them a very specific look at how the state standards are organized and assessed. It is, as I have noted earlier, essential that teachers understand the subskills used by the state to define reading, math, and any subject for which this work will be done. Also, it is important that teachers understand the weight given in the state assessments to the various subskills. If vocabulary is 24 percent of the total reading score, task force members need to know that. This document and the discussion it will encourage will help teachers better understand this essential piece of the puzzle. The answers to the questions posed in the discussion guide in the Power Standards Document Search box will vary from state to state in deference to the different documents available in the various states, but this guide will focus the group's discussion on the documents and information available.

It is now time to begin the discussion of the creation of local Power Standards based on the state standards. A review of Doug Reeves's essential components of Power Standards is in order. Doug Reeves suggests using the following three criteria to select standards that become the basis of Power Standards:

1. *Endurance:* Will the standard provide students with knowledge and skills beyond a single test date?

2. *Leverage:* Will the standard provide knowledge and skills that are of value in multiple disciplines?

3. *Readiness for the next level of learning:* Will the standard provide students with essential knowledge and skills that are necessary for their success in the next grade level?

In addition to these three criteria, I always add two more very important criteria.

As seen in the questionnaire in the Power Standards Document Search box, I want to make sure the task force considers what the state assesses and in what proportion it assesses those specific skills. If a single subskill makes up 24 percent of a state assessment, it is imperative that the task force know and consider that in the creation of Power Standards. This just makes good, common sense. Every state develops its own state standards and assessments that reflect very different parts of the skill called "reading." How the specific state defines and measures the skill broadly defined as reading absolutely must be taken into consideration in the development of the Power Standards. Again, this knowledge allows teachers to focus instruction on those skills deemed important by the state in the development of its assessments. This will further focus instruction on specific subskills within the skill defined as reading. It is very difficult for a teacher to design lessons around reading; however, a standard of drawing inference from text gives teachers the focus they need to design aligned instruction.

The other criteria I always use is to ask, What do we, as professional educators, *know* that our children must know and be able to do. The first-grade teacher, or the teacher of any grade or subject, who has devoted years of his or her life to teaching children needs to be able to include, or at least open to discussion by the group, those things that the teacher absolutely believes are an essential part of the important learnings that must occur in his or her specific grade level or content area. This acknowledging of professional experience and dedication goes a long way toward validating teachers and their experiences and helps draw everyone into the process.

Now that it is time to go to work, I always begin this section of the work with the following passage to once again focus the group on the work to be done. It usually takes about five minutes of silent reading time, but it really draws the group together on the task at hand.

WHAT ARE POWER STANDARDS, AND HOW DO THEY WORK?

In our current standards-based age of accountability with No Child Left Behind and mandatory state testing with dire consequences for schools with underperforming subgroups, many educators are overwhelmed by the sheer size and complexity of state and/or common core standards. Each state has its own standards, but all are complex and difficult to understand. We will follow the work of Doug Reeves and others by looking at this complex list of state standards and determining those standards that are truly the most important, most critical skills for our students to learn. While the complete list of all state and/or common core standards is overwhelming, further study and concentration can boil these down to the most important, most critical skills, which will become the basis of our instruction. These Power Standards then become the basis for all instruction and assessment and provide the kind of laser-like focus the school or district needs to provide a quality program for all kids.

The process of developing Power Standards is one of cooperation and professional judgments made by local teachers based on the state standards, assessment system, and what they know is best for kids. It usually requires one or two days to develop the Power Standards and requires a representative sample of teachers and administrators to do the work and then share that work with colleagues. Representative samples of teachers and administrators must include professionals from all grade levels and from as many schools as possible. Typically this work is done by groups of grade-level or course-specific teachers and then shared with grade levels or courses above and below that group's to ensure an appropriate academic fit. These groups will look at the state standards in their entirety, any other state documents (i.e., blueprints or whatever) to see if further clarification is available, and the state assessment documents to see what is tested. The group will then temper all of that with the group's own best judgment about what is best for our kids.

(Continued)

(Continued)

Once the Power Standards are developed and shared, the next step is the development of Quarterly Instructional Objectives. These instructional objectives answer the question, If this is the Power Standard (end-of-year skill), what will I need to teach my kids first quarter, second quarter, and so on? These are very specific instructional objectives that give very precise information to other teachers about exactly what will be taught during the quarterly time frame. Again, these are developed by representative teams, frequently the same teams that developed the Power Standards, and require about one to two days to develop.

The next step in this logical progression is the development of common quarterly assessments designed to measure student progress toward mastery of the Power Standards at every grade level and in all courses. The work on these assessments is generally begun in large groups to ensure all are clear about the directions and expectations. The work is usually done through extra-duty assignments or release time so that each group can pursue its specific work in a calmer, more focused environment, with the group coming back together to share and review work prior to implementation. This work is sometimes called "unpacking" the standards. The sources for these assessment items are usually released items from the state assessment, textbook assessment materials (but not chapter tests in total), teacher-developed assessments, and other sources.

The last leg of this journey is developing a system to use all of this data to improve instruction and learning. We must begin to use this entire package of formative assessments and other data to generate leading indicators of student performance that will affect student performance on the state's yearly mandatory summative assessment. These yearly high-stakes assessments are in reality trailing indicators of student performance, as Larry Lezotte points out, and can do little to affect student performance as they are generated after the assessment. We will be developing and learning to use leading indicators to drive instruction to improve student performance. These activities will give us the kind of curriculum alignment that research shows improves student performance through focusing on a specific curriculum that is aligned to the state assessment.

The document in the What Are Power Standards, and How Do They Work? box helps focus the group on the task at hand—developing our own local Power Standards. It also gives them a *Readers Digest* view of the entire process once again to ensure their understanding of what they will be doing. Following this reading, a brief discussion is held to help everyone understand the total process. Now it is time to begin the development process. Further, the Training and Resource Manual that I use in my formal training with school districts can be used for the work of this task force.

DEVELOPING POWER STANDARDS

It is now time for a discussion of the specific steps to take in developing our own local Power Standards. Shown in the Standards to Power Standards Discussion Guide box is the discussion guide used by the group to develop the Power Standards. After going through this document in detail, discussing every step, and answering questions, a copy is given to every member of the group, and the work begins.

STANDARDS TO POWER STANDARDS DISCUSSION GUIDE

1. Look at the list of standards, benchmarks, and content standards.
2. Look at the state assessments and No Child Left Behind Act—for what are we as educators being held accountable?
3. Determine the skill (noun) students are expected to master and what they are to do with that skill (verb).
4. Determine the most important, most critical skills to demonstrate mastery of the state standard.
5. Can these be combined with other skills to create a more singular Power Standard element?
6. How many skills are so critical that they need to be included in the Power Standard elements?
7. What is the maximum number of Power Standard elements that will give our colleagues the instructional focus to ensure student mastery?
8. Write the Power Standard elements, and relate those elements to specific state goals—remember, a learnable amount.

This is not necessarily a linear process in which the group completes number 1, then number 2, and so forth. The group will go through the discussion guide and consider the points as they are introduced and then refer back to them as needed or requested. This is an exceptionally exciting process to observe as caring, professional educators come together, often for the first time in their entire professional careers, to decide what it is that all students really must know and be able to do. It can be incredibly exciting, and passions can flare, but that is okay. Teachers feel passionate about what they are trying to teach their students, and it is often the first time they have ever really had a chance to discuss these issues. Allow these passionate discussions to go on, but the Project Owner must be available and ensure these discussions remain respectful and professional.

Item 8 on the discussion guide is there for those districts that wish to include the specific state and/or common core standards used in the development of their local Power Standards. Due to the number and complexity of some state standards, some educators feel compelled to reference those state standards in the development of their local Power Standards. That is why item 8 is included as an optional step. Resource B has samples of local Power Standards. I like to use the specific state standard used in developing the Power Standard to further demonstrate alignment.

Another important part of this discussion is the necessity of determining how the state defines the skill being assessed. Reading is a hugely important skill, to be sure. The questions are, How does this specific state define and measure student performance in reading? What subskills define reading? To what extent is each subskill judged to be important in measuring reading? For example, what percentage of the state assessment items is devoted to vocabulary? Twenty percent of the assessment questions? Thirty percent? Is drawing inference an important part of the assessments? These issues, in my opinion and in my experience, must be discussed and considered as part of the discussion of Power Standards. If vocabulary accounts for 28 percent of the items on a state assessment, teachers need to know that as they consider the most important standards that students must know and be able to do to be judged proficient on the state assessment.

The same holds true for math. What are the subskills the state has identified in defining math? Is algebraic reasoning a subskill? How about number sense? How does the state operationalize the subskills at each grade level? If, for example, geometric thinking accounts for 30 percent of the assessment items, teachers need to know that as they attempt to align instruction to assessment. To adequately prepare students for the state assessment, the teachers must first understand that state assessment system. Educators can argue until hell freezes over about whether the state assessment is fair or not, but it is the only system we currently have, so educators need to work within that system to help students be successful.

These curriculum discussions to determine the real curriculum that everyone will be expected to follow are hugely important discussions and can emit great passion and excitement. That is okay—it is important that teachers believe strongly in the things they teach. But what matters is participants' willingness to work together on those issues. The process of educators' coming to consensus about what are the most critical skills for kids to know and be able to do is far more important than the initial product they will produce. The initial product is a starting point, and that product will improve as it is aligned to the other grade levels and courses and is used, refined, and improved through the continuous improvement processes.

As the groups work, the Project Owner can move around the room to help, encourage, answer questions, and so forth. A hugely important part of this discussion is that the teachers in the various grade levels and departments are really internalizing the state standards—that is, coming to understand them at a much deeper level than they have ever done in the past, if they have ever even dealt with the state standards before. This process requires time (most groups I have worked with complete their Power Standards about halfway through the first day and begin the Quarterly Instructional Objectives before the end of the first day), facilitation, and patience. Teachers are accustomed to having the correct answer and being absolutely sure of that correct answer. This process does not provide such clear-cut, obviously correct answers. As has been stated throughout this book—process over product. The process of educators' coming together to come to consensus on such important matters is the important piece here. The product will improve as it goes through the continuous improvement loop, over and over again.

> It is during this discussion phase that the group must come to understand the communicative intent of the Power Standards. These Power Standards must give your colleagues the specific detail they need to know to define the exact learnings for which their students will be accountable. I frequently say, "If you got hit by a truck tomorrow, would your colleagues be able to look at the Power Standards and know exactly what it is their students are supposed to know and be able to do?" It is a rather graphic question, but it helps focus participants' efforts.

It is also during these discussions that I will frequently say, "Thank goodness for Plan, Do, Check, Act!" Any commitment or decision made will be subject to the Plan, Do, Check, Act cycle and therefore up for yearly review and revision. If the group agrees to try something, it is with the full understanding that it, like all group decisions, will be subject to the continuous improvement loop of Plan, Do, Check, Act. Once people understand that an issue or approach will be tried and evaluated to see if it works, then most people are willing to give it a try.

During this writing phase of the process, some groups will finish their first draft before others. As the Project Owner moves around the room, encourage those groups that finish sooner to share their work to help other groups. This can be as simple as putting the Power Standard on an overhead projector to share with the entire group. This sample is not put up as an exemplar or as the correct answer but rather as an important measure in the group learning process so that everyone can learn from one another. As the Power Standard is shared, it is a perfect opportunity to discuss why this skill or standard is included and why that skill or standard is not. Allow the process to flow freely, and let everyone participate and learn.

The software developed by and available from Partners4results (and demonstrated at www.partners4results.org/demo) allows all of this work to happen on the Internet. All writing, editing, sharing, and publishing of the Power Standards is done on this Internet-based software, and the work is then available for use, viewing, and publication over the Internet. This gives members and nonmembers of the task force 24-7 access to the work for sharing and electronic discussion purposes, which goes a long way toward expediting and supporting the process.

This development of Power Standards aligned to the state and/or common core standards and agreed to across a single grade level is usually referred to as "horizontal alignment" or "alignment across the grade level." The teachers gathered in this group must come to consensus about exactly what it is that all children must know and be able to do as a result of the school experience in a particular grade level or course. The key concept here is that educators, as a profession, must agree on the key, common learnings in third grade, in algebra, or in any other learning before the system can hold kids accountable for that learning.

An important part of this process is the numbering system for the Power Standards. This will help everyone easily identify the Power Standards and will be most helpful as the process moves through the Quarterly Instructional Objectives and common assessments. Every Power Standard should be identified with a number (for grade level) and a letter (for subject). Thus, the eighth-grade math Power Standard will be 8M, third-grade reading will be 3R, and so on. At the department level, the course name replaces the number and letter. Algebra I is labeled AlgI, A1, or whatever the system agrees to, and so on. This makes every Power Standard readily identifiable for future reference and work. Again, this numbering system is electronically applied by those using the Partners4results software package.

As the task force develops these specific Power Standards, bring the entire work group together to share these initial attempts across all participants to ensure vertical articulation across grade levels and courses. It works well to begin with math as an example and to allow each grade level to share its Power Standards with the entire group. One by one, each grade level shares its first draft of the Power Standards, and the entire group gets to ask clarifying questions—What does this mean? Do you realize you excluded number sense? This gives all participants a chance to see other work and expand their own thinking at their own grade level. This is also a great time to discuss form and format. What format will we choose as our "official" format? Bullets? Paragraphs? Does it matter? Will we list the state standards used in developing the Power Standards? Unless otherwise determined, these are matters of local preference and may be decided by the group at this phase or at some other time in the discussion.

Once the grade-level groups believe they have completed the design of their own grade-level Power Standards, the task force must take the time for the vertical articulation piece—that is, is there a natural flow of skills that reflect a logical sequence of learnings and expectations for students from grade level to grade level or from course to course? During this phase of the process, it is best to have each grade level or course in an academic sequence meet with the grade level or course that is above it and below it in the sequencing of courses or grades. That is, the first grade will meet with the kindergarten and second grades, one at a time, and each grade level will share its first draft of the Power Standards for the grade level. The same will happen with the Algebra I and Algebra II groups, and so on for every sequenced course in the building/district. This very important step allows teachers to see their own work in light of the expectations of the teachers who provide their students and the teachers to whom they will send their own students the following year or course. By sharing partially completed or first-draft work, the process allows groups to learn from each other.

Larry Ainsworth (2003a) suggests having groups meet in K–2, 3–5, and 6–8 configurations. Based on my previous work, this works well, as does the single-grade-level articulation. You can decide based on the size of the district and task force. However, it is essential to address this vertical articulation issue before the Power Standards are finalized. Local leadership may or may not choose to use the consultant to facilitate the discussions about vertical articulation; however, leaders do need to ensure this vertical articulation conversation is held.

This phase of the project can be somewhat chaotic as there may be as many as eight or ten intergrade-level/departmental meetings going on at the same time. Tolerate and enjoy the noise. You are providing an exchange between professionals that will define exactly those skills that students will be required to learn. It is very exciting. It is not at all unusual to hear the third-grade teacher say to the second-grade teacher, "If you will be sure the kids learn that in second grade, I will stop worrying about it in third grade," and on up the grade levels and departments as teachers finally come to consensus about what the expected learnings are in each grade level and course. It is exciting and professionally fulfilling to provide such an important forum for the exchange of such important ideas.

Now that the task force has done the horizontal and vertical articulation work, each grade level or department should be given time to review and revise its work one more time prior to final submission for publication to ensure it represents the group's very best work. Some people will still be anxious about whether they have their Power Standards exactly perfect. The reality is, there is never a perfect product, so we will apply the Plan, Do, Check, Act cycle to continuously improve the Power Standards. Remember, thank goodness for Plan, Do, Check, Act.

A question that is frequently asked is, What if the task force develops a weak Power Standard that is not truly aligned to the state standard? This question is usually answered during the horizontal or vertical articulation meetings. As groups of teachers look at the Power Standards and apply the questions and critical attributes, changes are inevitably made to the Power Standards needing change and improvement. If these issues are not identified during this initial articulation process, the distribution process with the mandatory feedback loop and the quarterly feedback forms will generally bring the problem areas into focus. Again, we have to meet the teachers and their knowledge base where they are (just like our classroom learners) and help them grow into the higher levels of understanding through this process.

DEPLOYING THE POWER STANDARDS

It is now time for a very important part of the project—deploying these curriculum documents to the entire district staff, we must formally commit to (1) who will do what, (2) when that work will be due, and (3) what will happen to that work once it is done. The task force defines this work process to ensure those commitments really happen:

- There is an actual plan, known by and shared with all the participants, that specifically outlines the work to be done and the due dates for the work.
- Who will do that work and how they will share that work with others is clearly defined.
- In what format the work will be done and submitted (electronically, in Word, Excel, whatever) is clearly defined.
- This plan ensures that the Plan, Do, Check, Act cycle will be followed in completing this project.
- The task force defines the actual process to be followed and the specific steps and deadlines to ensure Plan, Do, Check, Act is followed.
- Feedback on the Power Standards will be gathered and processed by the task force, and the dates and responsibilities for that work are clearly defined.
- The results of the feedback on the Power Standards will be processed and shared with the district staff to keep everyone involved in the process.

Below is the form used to gather this information for task force use. It is like the other forms from the Training and Resource manual in that spaces have been deleted for ease of publishing.

FOLLOW-UP PROCESS GUIDELINES: POWER STANDARDS

This group may not answer all of these questions today. We should begin the discussion today and develop a process with dates to ensure this work gets decided and completed. With time and commitment, this will become part of a yearly cycle that will ensure the curriculum is always under review and continually improved. The first year or so will be a bit more difficult as timelines are set and processes for review and revision are established. Please be patient and help by being part of the solution. Share your ideas and help us continually improve. The Plan cycle was completed by the work of this group; now we must make sure we follow up with the Do, Check, and Act cycles.

Do Cycle

- When will the Power Standards be due?
- To whom?
- In what format? Electronic? On a form?
- What will they look like? Decide now or later.
- Will the task force/faculty see them prior to final publication? When? Meeting called by whom?
- When will they be published and distributed to staff? By whom? Any follow-up activity by the task force as part of the distribution?

Check Cycle

- When will we gather initial feedback on the Power Standards?
- Who will gather and collate?
- Will we allow midcourse corrections or stick with the initial product for the first year?
- When will we gather end-of-year feedback? From whom? How?

Act Cycle

- When will we meet to review the feedback and make improvements and corrections?
- When and how will we release this second version (and subsequent versions)?

The real beauty of this step in the process, and the issue that most participants find refreshing (and often out of character for the system), is that the system commits to do the work and provide accountabilities to see that it gets done. This form and the discussions it generates share a very important commitment with everyone that the work will be followed up on and that it will not just end up on a shelf somewhere. The system will follow through to make sure this happens.

PUBLISHING THE POWER STANDARDS

After deploying the Power Standards, the task force decides if its work is complete and the Power Standards are ready for submission for publication. That decision is based on how much progress has been made, but the Follow-Up Process Guidelines: Power Standards form will ensure there is a timeline for completing, submitting, and distributing the work. Exactly when the work is submitted and ready for initial publication needs to be determined. Following the initial development and publication of the Power Standards, if time permits, a follow-up task force session may be scheduled to check the Power Standards one last time prior to final distribution to the entire staff. The task force may decide to review them again for vertical articulation, that is, articulation from grade level to grade level and course to course (e.g., Algebra I to Algebra II). The progress of the group will help in making this decision.

It is during the initial review process and the second review for vertical articulation that the groups must look for gaps, overlaps, and omissions as well as an appropriate fit among grade levels. Do these Power Standards cover all of the most important learnings for students? Is there a logical sequencing of skills between grade levels and courses that educators believe will work? Did the group include the major concepts covered in the state standards that are deemed important?

Once the Power Standards have been developed and reviewed, including an examination for vertical articulation, they are ready for publication and distribution to the entire staff. If time permits, it is especially helpful for this almost-finished product, that is, the list of Power Standards developed by the task force, to be shared with the entire faculty by grade level or specific courses for the faculty's input prior to finalization, publication, and use in the building/district. The proposed Power Standards in first grade, for example, should be shared with all first-grade teachers prior to final publication and implementation, with an opportunity for all first-grade teachers to have input into the product. All must feel they had a chance for input into the process so some sense of ownership is created.

Time may be a factor here as the approach of the school year may preclude sharing with the entire staff over the summer, but the Power Standards can be published and shared with the entire staff as part of the opening school activities in August or September. They can be distributed for discussion at staff meetings, with the feedback forms returned to the task force by the date determined on the Follow-Up Process Guidelines: Power Standards. The task force will make decisions in a realistic, doable way so the work can be done and shared as best the school/district can. The important issue here, and throughout the entire process, is that every effort to share and get feedback from the professional staff be made.

GATHERING FEEDBACK

During this initial distribution of the Power Standards, it is a particularly great time to review the entire project with the staff members to make sure they understand where the initiative is going and their role in that initiative. The process of developing Power Standards is only one phase of the entire project. This is also a great time to introduce the members of the task force (and thank them for their work and contributions) and to let everyone on the staff know what has happened and what will be happening. This project should have been well planned and discussed throughout the district as it moved toward implementation, so this should not be brand new information to anyone, but sharing and reviewing is always helpful. You cannot overcommunicate on an issue that is this important.

Shown in the Power Standards Feedback box is another form and proposed memo used to gather feedback from the staff during this initial distribution phase; I have removed spaces for ease of publishing. It shows the attempt to gather feedback from the entire professional staff and looks at very specific issues:

- Do staff members understand the concept of Power Standards?
- Do they know what to do with those Power Standards?
- Do they believe they can do that?
- Do they believe the students are capable of learning these Power standards?
- Are they willing to help?

Knowing these specific issues will help the task force and building leadership direct their specific staff development plans. If teachers don't understand Power Standards, then the staff development issue is decided— help them understand this critical curriculum document. The same holds true for all of the questions. Use this specific feedback to design appropriate staff development.

POWER STANDARDS FEEDBACK

Attached please find copies of our new district Power Standards. These are our very own Power Standards and will serve as the basis for all instruction in our district. These Power Standards were developed by a task force of teachers and are based on national research to improve student performance. If we are to move all of our children forward and meet the mandates of No Child Left Behind, we must standardize these curriculum expectations across the district. To make sure that everyone understands his or her role in this implementation process, we are asking your help to provide us feedback on our work and share your needs for staff development as we implement these new standards.

(Continued)

(Continued)

Please complete the feedback sheet below and return it to your principal by [DATE]. He or she will forward it to [NAME] for use by the task force at its next meeting. Any questions may be directed to your principal or a member of the task force. Thank you for your help in this exciting endeavor.

1 is bad—5 is good.

1. I understand the Power Standards.

1	2	3	4	5
Strongly Disagree	Disagree	Neutral	Agree	Strongly Agree

Comments (use back of page if needed):

2. I understand what I am expected to do with the new Power Standards and Quarterly Instructional Objectives.

1	2	3	4	5
Strongly Disagree	Disagree	Neutral	Agree	Strongly Agree

Comments (use back of page if needed):

3. I believe I am capable of teaching the Power Standards.

1	2	3	4	5
Strongly Disagree	Disagree	Neutral	Agree	Strongly Agree

Comments (use back of page if needed):

4. I believe our students are capable of learning these Power Standards in the grade level to which these standards are assigned.

1	2	3	4	5
Strongly Disagree	Disagree	Neutral	Agree	Strongly Agree

Comments (use back of page if needed):

5. I would be willing to volunteer to work with the Power Standards task force to continue and improve this work.

1	2	3	4	5
Strongly Disagree	Disagree	Neutral	Agree	Strongly Agree

Comments (use back of page if needed):

Grade Level: _____ Building: _____

Signature (Optional): _____

Options You May Want to Include in This Memo

- List members of the Power Standards task force and their home schools/ departments. If you do list them, please make sure you thank them for their hard work and commitment to the project.
- List the date, time, and location of the next meeting of the task force to provide a sense of importance in the timing of the return of the feedback and/or to encourage attendance as observers or participants in that meeting.
- Date when it is expected the next version of the Power Standards will be distributed to the entire staff for implementation for the coming year.

Once the Power Standards Feedback sheets are received by the task force, several things must happen to that feedback. It will be gathered first by building if there is more than one building in the district. The building principal must collect and collate these feedback sheets. This will give the building principal very specific information about the staff's knowledge of and comfort with the Power Standards. The principal must then take very specific steps to address the concerns expressed by the staff. These should be viewed as internal, building concerns, best addressed at the building level by building leadership. I like the use of the optional signature—it allows staff members to include their names or not as they deem appropriate. There are times we definitely want people to know how we feel about an issue.

The principal may feel he or she needs some backup support or expertise provided by members of the task force or the Project Owner, and that should be provided if needed. However, the building principal cannot take the attitude, "This is central office's (or whoever's) project, and I don't know anything about it. Don't ask me, I only work here." It is time for the instructional leader to be the instructional leader and help everyone understand the expectation. There should be members of the task force in the building, and the principal may have even worked on one of the grade-level or department groups. Work together to find solutions and help people understand and work together.

All of this feedback is then gathered by the Project Owner as outlined in the Follow-Up Process Guidelines: Power Standards form used earlier. This collated feedback from the district staff is shared with the district staff—it is critical that every member of the staff know how the entire staff feels. It is a completely different issue if one or two people are unhappy with an initiative than if 50 percent of the staff is unhappy. Leaders, as well as everyone else, need to know the depth and breadth of the satisfaction or dissatisfaction so they may address it accordingly. If the steps outlined in this book were followed, the staff resistance should have been minimized, but sometimes old wounds cause current issues. Identify and deal with those issues, but the entire staff needs to know how the entire staff feels about the initiative. Remember, data create a picture of your current reality.

The task force will then meet to discuss the feedback and make decisions. A meeting for the Power Standards task force by grade level or department is usually the best way to do this. This meeting to consider staff input must be publicized and its results shared with all teachers so that everyone knows that the thoughts and feelings of the entire staff have been considered by the Power Standards task force. In a relatively small district that has involved the entire district in developing the Power Standards, this step may not be necessary.

Another important issue to make crystal clear is that while the task force receives input and ideas from the larger group, the task force decides what changes or additions will be made to the Power Standards prior to finalization and publishing. The task force will consider all input, but it is the task force's decision, in the end, as to what will be included in the final product. Since these task forces are primarily teachers, the entire staff may rest assured that the initiative was teacher controlled, yet it is imperative that everyone understand who will make the final decision. Nobody can argue over an issue forever. Sooner or later, the group must come to consensus and move the project forward. This should have been discussed during the goals, roles, and responsibilities section of the process.

A way to measure the needs of the building administrators is to use the form in the Instructional Leadership Talking Points box to guide an interview. This form is from the Resource and Training Manual and is used as needed to ensure building administrators are given the resources they need. As with the other forms, spaces have been deleted for ease of publishing.

This form may be used by the Project Owner to interview building administrators to gather their input and make sure the project is understood and on track.

INSTRUCTIONAL LEADERSHIP TALKING POINTS

How is the project going in your building?

What data do you have, if any, to support that belief?

- Meetings?
- Conversations?
- Work product?

Are there any specific parts of the project that are going particularly well? Having particular issues?

- Power Standards?
- Quarterly Instructional Objectives?
- Intragrade-level cooperation?
- Intergrade-level cooperation?
- Publishing/sharing?
- Any department/grade-level issues?
- Other?

Are there any specific areas in which you need additional resources?

- Time?
- Training?
- Financial?
- Other?

Do you have any recommendations for continuation/elimination from the project timelines/guidelines?

- Deadlines?
- Work schedule?
- Work product?
- Forms?
- Other?

Is there any specific information/request you would like to share?

FINAL PUBLICATION AND USE OF POWER STANDARDS

It is now time to publish and distribute the Power Standards in final format for implementation throughout the building/district. When these are distributed to the entire building/district, it is critical that the expectations for their use be shared with everyone as well. Remember, the project will next move into the development of the Quarterly Instructional Objectives, so that issue must be shared as well. Make sure all participants know what they are expected to do with these documents so nobody gets off on a tangent.

It is envisioned that at this point the Power Standards are to be used as the central planning document for instruction, and teachers are to ensure that their instruction leads their students toward mastery of these Power Standards. Since every teacher knows the Quarterly Instructional Objectives are coming next, the deployment of the Power Standards can be very helpful in beginning and encouraging the conversations needed to develop the Quarterly Instructional Objectives. Don't be afraid to begin the discussion with, "If this is what we want students to know and be able to do by the end of the year/course, what must those students learn first quarter? Second?" These kinds of conversation will help the next phase of the project move forward more smoothly.

> Bloom found that most (but not all) of the perceived variability in student learning rates is really a function of the presence or absence of prerequisites.
>
> —Larry Lezotte (Lezotte & Cipriano Pepperl, 1999, p. 126)

PROCESS SUMMARY

The actual work of the task force has begun, so you are now leading the work and making sure the process is implemented as designed and that any issues that come up are addressed. The work of the task force can elicit strong emotions as dedicated professionals struggle to identify the most important standards for all students to learn. Your group facilitation skills, and sometimes being fast on your feet, are really important. Always remember that the things you design will be subject to the continuous improvement loop, so if they don't work as designed, they can and will be fixed as part of this process.

Political Issues

During this phase of the project, the local politics should already be taken care of as addressed in the group formation and selection. During the goals, roles, and responsibilities phase of the task force assignments, make sure none of the assigned goals, roles, or responsibilities conflict with local custom, teacher contract, state law, or practice. Make sure the teacher contract and/or past practice is followed relative to pay, assignments, extra duty, and so forth. As always, communication with the board, teachers, and community must be ongoing and completely honest.

Leadership Issues

The necessary major leadership skills will be group facilitation and keeping the group on task. Listen closely to and encourage the professional conversations about essential learnings to hear the direction in which the task force is moving, and make sure to keep participants on track. Help them avoid what Madelyn Hunter calls "bird walks" and rehashing past grievances.

Continuous Improvement Issues

The work of the group has begun, and total quality management tenets must be applied and used continuously from this point forward. You will share with the group the forms and processes to ensure continuous improvement and expected due dates for the use of the Plan, Do, Check, Act cycle throughout the project. The deliberate solicitation of the entire staff for feedback, the processing of that feedback by the task force, and the reporting back to the entire staff about decisions will be seriously addressed from this point forward. Remember, Plan, Do, Check, Act never ends—we are in this for the long haul to ensure continuous improvement. As discussed earlier, reflection is part of the Act cycle, so make sure people reflect on the feedback and make the appropriate decisions.

Technical Skills

You are into the process full swing now, so it is imperative to follow the technical steps outlined in the development of the Power Standards. These steps are predominantly linear at this point, so make sure to follow them in their predetermined order. This is a very exciting phase as the staff engages in the process of determining exactly what students must know and be able to do. Enjoy the excitement and the conversations.

PROCESS CHECKLIST

- ❏ Review the goals, roles, and responsibilities.
- ❏ Use the Power Standards Document Search form to ensure all members of the task force understand the state curriculum and assessment documents that they will be using.

(Continued)

(Continued)

☐ Share the article, "What Are Power Standards, and How Do They Work?"

☐ Ensure task force members understand the skill that is expected in the state standard (the noun or noun phrase) and the performance the students are expected to do with that skill (the verb).

☐ Develop the first draft of the Power Standards.

☐ Share those Power Standards drafts as they are developed.

☐ Allow for open and honest discussion as the work moves forward.

☐ Come to consensus by grade level/course on the Power Standards (horizontal articulation).

☐ Number each of the Power Standards.

☐ Share the Power Standards across grade levels/sequential courses (vertical articulation).

☐ Complete the Follow-Up Process Guidelines: Power Standards form.

☐ Share the commitments made on the Follow-Up Process Guidelines: Power Standards with the task force, and ensure these commitments are honored by the appropriate personnel.

☐ If there is time, distribute the initial draft of the Power Standards to the district staff for feedback prior to final publication. Whether this can be done will depend on when the work is finished and is not critical to success.

☐ Distribute the Power Standards Feedback form with the initial draft of the Power Standards to the entire district staff.

☐ Make sure the feedback results are collated and shared with everyone—the entire district staff and the task force.

☐ Make sure building principals are active in processing the feedback to ensure they understand and can help address issues raised by the staff.

☐ Decide whether you need to use the Instructional Leadership Talking Points form with your principals to measure their ability to deal with the initiative.

☐ Make sure the task force meets, if possible, to consider feedback and make final decisions about the Power Standards prior to their publication and use.

☐ Ensure those task force decisions are shared with the entire staff and the Power Standards are deployed throughout the building/district.

☐ Ensure the Plan, Do, Check, Act process is integrated into the Power Standards document as a yearly feedback/revision process.

☐ Ensure expectations for the use of Power Standards in planning instruction are made crystal clear to everyone.

☐ Prepare for the discussion about Quarterly Instructional Objectives.

4

The Next Step

Quarterly Instructional Objectives

CHAPTER EXPECTATIONS

This chapter explains the important publishing and communication issues involved in Power Standards and how to formulate Quarterly Instructional Objectives. A numbering system will be used for the Quarterly Instructional Objectives that will tie them to the Power Standards and the common assessments. By creating the energy and commitment to establish Power Standards, the hardest work is over, and this chapter outlines the steps needed to develop the Quarterly Instructional Objectives, which give the staff the specific focus to design instruction to enable students to master Power Standards. The chapter not only defines Quarterly Instructional Objectives and how to develop them but also shares sample Quarterly Instructional Objectives and discusses the publishing and communication opportunities they present.

THE CHANGE PROCESS CONTINUES

All right! By following the work in Chapter 3, you should now understand how to develop Power Standards for every grade level and every course taught in the building/district. Once implemented, those Power Standards will make a huge difference in teaching and learning.

The Power Standards may be the greatest document in the educational world, but if nobody in the local educational community knows about them, they will make no difference in the work of educating children. The potential of the Power Standards unfolds as they are distributed and used to change what students learn during their educational experience. As stated in total quality management, a mediocre strategy effectively deployed will produce better results than an effective strategy that is poorly deployed. So the challenge is to effectively deploy the Power Standards at all levels of the organization.

First and foremost, let's talk about deploying the Power Standards to the teaching staff. If the recommendations in Chapter 3 were followed, once the first draft was completed, Power Standards were distributed to the entire staff for input and feedback prior to final publishing. The horizontal and vertical articulation issues also were addressed, and everyone was given opportunities for feedback. The Power Standards are now ready for final distribution and, most important, ready for use to drive instruction. These Power Standards have been developed, reviewed, and approved by the building's/district's own professional staff, so the matter of buy-in has been addressed. The entire system must now implement the new program—it cannot be an option.

The change process is now at the stage of implementation wherein the entire system must do what was agreed to. This is sometimes referred to as DWYSYWD—do what you said you would do. The professional staff has discussed, debated, compromised, listened, spoken, and so forth. It is now time to implement. The entire teaching and administrative staff must be supportive of the Power Standards they created. They are to be faithfully implemented in each and every classroom in the building/district. Administrative support, in particular, cannot be an option. The ship of state, if you will, has decided on its direction, and internal leadership are expected to support that direction. If internal administrative leaders are not committed to moving the project forward, then the supervisors of those uncommitted administrators must do what is necessary to make sure all administrative and teaching staff faithfully implement the project or face the logical consequences.

PUBLISHING AND COMMUNICATION ISSUES

The Power Standards should be distributed in several formats for the various uses they will have. The publication of the complete set of Power Standards for the K–12 educational program is a logical first step. Based on the advice in Chapter 3, all Power Standards should be similarly formatted, so the final product should present a coordinated, well-articulated document for the entire educational community. This issue is tended to in the Partners4results software discussed in the Software Availability section, but those not using the software will need to tend to this issue.

The complete K–12 set of Power Standards should be published in sufficient quantity so that, if possible, every teacher in the system can have access to a complete set of the K–12 Power Standards. If this is not possible, then at a minimum, a complete set of K–12 Power Standards should be available for every grade level in a building and every department in a secondary setting. Copies should be made available in every building for administrators as well as in office areas, faculty lounges, work areas, and so forth. The size of the district may mandate that the complete set be housed electronically on the district website, and the Partners4results software will readily house these curriculum documents on the Internet. This electronic, Internet posting is a great idea even in smaller districts as it allows ready access by the community to this important document.

Also, the work of publishing this document should be assigned to a single office (the Project Owner's) and a single person who has demonstrated his or her publishing and layout skills in previous work. As well as being the primary curriculum document for the district, this document will serve as a primary communication and public relations document, and its appearance and layout must be impeccable. A short introductory letter from the superintendent or Project Owner explaining its use and importance is also a nice touch. Make sure this publishing expectation is understood from the onset of the project so there are no surprises or anger as the project moves into the publication phase. As discussed in Chapter 3, there is software and Internet hosting available for this process and these documents from www.partners4results.org.

If all Power Standards are submitted electronically in Microsoft Word, it will be relatively easy for the person in charge of publishing to reformat the Power Standards into the district format and publish them. Also, the district logo should appear in a common place so that the document is readily identified with the district.

The complete set of Power Standards should also be available for all of the constituents in the district. Parents, visitors, and prospective residents who are looking at the quality of the educational programming will be impressed by a singular, focused document that clearly defines expected learnings in the entire building/district. Leadership should take full advantage of the Power Standards as a public relations document to communicate the educational vision.

Another way to publish the grade-level Power Standards is as single-page documents for use by classroom teachers in every grade level or course. These grade-level or course-specific Power Standards may be given to students at the beginning of the year, sent to parents as part of the welcome-to-the-new-class materials, distributed at open houses, sent home in students' Friday packets, or whatever. Besides communicating student learning expectations for the year, these one-page documents show the serious commitment of staff to work together to identify those learnings and articulate expectations. Parents with more than one child in the system cannot help but be impressed by multiple documents in the same format for each of their children in various grade levels and courses. It demonstrates the district's commitment to coordinated, aligned teaching and learning.

Further, these grade-level or course-specific documents give the students, especially those in the higher grade levels, exact information about what they are expected to learn while in the class for the year, helping to demystify the learning and reduce student anxiety. Remember, research shows that when students know the expected learning in advance of the instruction, performance is improved.

The building principal will want to gather the Power Standards for every grade level or course in the building into a single folder or handout for use in the main office. Again, this is a powerful communication and public relations tool for prospective parents, visitors, real estate agents, and so forth because this document clearly demonstrates the district's commitment to following national research. The local system has created curriculum documents that clearly define learning in the building. Why not share those documents and let everyone know how serious and competent the building/district is at its work?

Several of the districts I have worked with also enlarge one-page Power Standards to poster size for posting in the individual classrooms. This, again, conveys the focus of classroom instruction and defines the expected learnings. Like all publishing, the poster publishing work must be a district or building responsibility rather than a classroom teacher expectation. It can be done by a local commercial printer or with one of the new poster printers available for office use. It is hoped that teachers are too busy facilitating student learning to undertake this project, and they may not have the resources or expertise the office staff has for this kind of work. The consistent appearance of these documents across buildings and the entire district sends a powerful message to everyone about the focus of the district.

It is almost impossible to overcommunicate, so give building principals and teachers some leeway in going beyond the district expectations and exercising their own creativity in publishing and distributing. They know the students well and have been effectively communicating with parents for years; allow them to use that talent to improve this effort. Then provide a forum to discuss ways others have found to better communicate and share the Power Standards. Remember, Plan, Do, Check, Act—see how the process is working and what can be done to improve it. People love a chance to demonstrate their own competence and creativity to their peers.

BOARD OF EDUCATION ACTION

Whether the Board of Education approves or adopts curriculum for the district can be a contentious issue for some districts. Whatever past practice and local politics dictate should be followed in this decision. Whether or not the decision is made to have the board officially adopt this work, it is important that the board know what work has been done.

The Power Standards can be taken to the school board, explained, voted on, and accepted by the Board of Education as the official curriculum documents for the building/district, if that is what is traditionally done. This achieves several purposes. It presents, in a relatively compact document, the entire scope and sequence of the K–12 educational expectations and shows that the educational experience is aligned to the state standards. Remember, the Power Standards for a single grade level (including all subjects) should not exceed one page, and Power Standards for specific courses will be significantly less than a page. They encapsulate the most critical, most important learnings for the entire district into a single, readable, understandable, and—most important—learnable document that speaks volumes to the board and community about the focus of the district's educational program.

Also, adoption or some form of formal acceptance by the Board of Education makes the Power Standards an official curriculum document backed up by the force of law. The Power Standards are not just an idea from central office or the flavor of the month but rather a formal document adopted by the Board of Education with the expectation that the Power Standards will be fully implemented in every classroom in the district. This makes teachers and the entire community realize the importance and permanence of these Power Standards.

THE GROUP TO DO THE WORK

Many of the issues previously discussed regarding group membership will apply to the group doing the work of creating the Quarterly Instructional Objectives. In fact, many districts use the same people to develop Power Standards and Quarterly Instructional Objectives. This makes perfect sense in most cases. The group has found common ground, established relationships, and learned to work together effectively. The Project Owner, however, may also use the transition from developing the Power Standards to developing the Quarterly Instructional Objectives to facilitate change in the task force structure or membership as he or she deems necessary. This is an ideal time to make such changes.

The goals, roles, and responsibilities should be reviewed and updated, and the reporting formats and dates decided on and communicated. For further clarification, please review the Goals, Roles, and Responsibilities, and Who Will Do the Work, and What Will They Do? sections in Chapter 2. Further, there may be personnel changes in critical positions due to resignations, retirements, and so forth. That is why it has been stressed that this is a process without assigned roles. If someone leaves the district or the task force, a replacement is found and brought up to speed with where the task force is, and the work continues. None of us is so critical to the process that he or she cannot be replaced.

WHAT ARE QUARTERLY INSTRUCTIONAL OBJECTIVES?

The next step in this alignment process is the development of the Quarterly Instructional Objectives, but what are Quarterly Instructional Objectives? Very simply put—to achieve Power Standards by the end of the year, what must students learn during the first quarter? Second quarter? Third quarter? Fourth quarter? These are the questions that the Quarterly Instructional Objectives will answer. Quarterly Instructional Objectives tell the teachers (and the students) exactly what students need to learn to master the Power Standards.

The use of the Quarterly Instructional Objectives, which are based on the Power Standards, clearly defines for the teacher (and the student) the specific instructional objectives he or she needs to cover to ensure the students master the Power Standards. Quarterly Instructional Objectives very clearly define which specific skills must be learned, and in what order they must be learned, to master the Power Standards. Like the Power Standards on which the Quarterly Instructional Objectives are based, these quarterly expectations are developed through discussions among the staff and then improved through the Plan, Do, Check, Act cycle.

It is important to understand that the Quarterly Instructional Objectives are based on the Power Standards, which in turn are based on the state and/or common core standards, not the chapters in the textbook. This means teachers will design instruction around the state and/or common core standards (through the Power Standards and Quarterly Instructional Objectives), not the textbook's chapter sequence or some curriculum document that expects complete textbook coverage in an attempt to cover all of the state standards. This is huge! As education moves into a standards-based curriculum, as discussed in previous chapters, content must become a means to a performance end. Teachers teach the standard (Power Standard) and break that instruction into component skills in a well-articulated sequence that maximizes student learning.

Further, it must be emphasized that these Quarterly Instructional Objectives cannot be long lists of specific skills that are so inclusive and so definitive that they present a totally unteachable or unassessable curriculum document. We cannot have forty-four or some such huge number of

Quarterly Instructional Objectives that will have the teacher trying to deftly dance through all of them and then build assessments that are too long or too involved to realistically be taught and assessed in the time assigned. Remember, we are creating a learnable curriculum. We can teach the entire textbook; kids just can't learn the entire textbook in one year. The sample Quarterly Instructional Objectives in this chapter and those at www.partners4results.org/demo demonstrate this.

Every state defines reading, math, and every other content area through various specific subskills or component parts. Reading, for example, has subskills that vary from state to state. Vocabulary may account for 24 percent of the state assessment in one state and as little as 10 percent in another state. What other subskills or component skills are used in the state's definition of reading, and in what proportion are these included in the state assessment? As in the design of the Power Standards, that information guides the development of the Quarterly Instructional Objectives.

Quarterly Instructional Objectives clearly define and limit what students must learn. They also force teachers to agree on when to cover specific skills to optimize student learning. Teachers are no longer expected to cover the entire book or some all-inclusive document that teachers can teach but the kids can never learn. Nor are teachers free to develop their own sequencing calendar or base their instruction on personal preferences. As professional educators, teachers have examined the state standards, come to consensus on the most important and most critical learnings, and now will work together to develop Quarterly Instructional Objectives to further define and clarify that expected learning.

> During this phase of the process, I frequently brag to the group that I taught my dog to whistle. As they look at me curiously, and I repeat my claim to fame, they really don't get it. Then I share the fact that the dog never learned it, but I taught it. That is unfortunately the case with much of what we teach kids. We can and do teach the entire book; unfortunately, the kids don't learn it. That is the source of much of our problem. We teach too much, and the kids can't learn it that fast.

These Quarterly Instructional Objectives are vaguely similar to what many districts call pacing guides or instructional focus calendars, but there are several very important distinctions. The Quarterly Instructional Objectives are based on the Power Standards, those standards deemed to be the most important things for students to know and be able to do. Quarterly Instructional Objectives further extend the identification and definition of those most critical, most important learnings to specific skills that must be mastered and, in many cases, in what order they must be mastered. Additionally, the Quarterly Instructional Objectives are quarterly expectations, much broader in scope than the weekly or even daily instructional focus calendar or pacing guide expectations used by some buildings/districts, allowing more flexibility and room for unexpected issues such as snow days, learning differences, substitutes, and emergency closings.

In the formal training for developing these Quarterly Instructional Objectives, I frequently define the critical attributes (à la Madelyn Hunter) as the following: they

- clearly define expected learning at the appropriate contextual level,
- are assessable—you CAN write items to measure that skill,
- are the basis for lesson design,
- are presented in understandable language—share with kids and parents,
- represent a learnable amount for the quarter, and
- are in the need-to-know, not the nice-to-know, category.

Again, it is absolutely essential to understand that these Power Standards and Quarterly Instructional Objectives define the *what* of student learning, not the *how* of teaching. These Power Standards and Quarterly Instructional Objectives are not dictating or even discussing how the material will be taught—that is the job, gift, and science of the classroom teacher. Quarterly Instructional Objectives define the learning, not the methodology.

A CURRICULUM SYSTEM

It is critical for the district to agree on what will be taught and when it will be taught to ensure a common curriculum that can be measured and improved. As long as the instructional sequence and content are left to chance or the choice of individual teachers, no matter how well intentioned those efforts are, no curriculum system is in place; rather, a series of random actions is in place. Under such an unaligned "system," one can look only at disparate student performance results and speculate as to the causes of differences. This alignment process allows for the development of a curriculum system that is used by all instructional staff, and only a system can affect all of the children.

Standardization of the curriculum, that is, ensuring all students learn the same skills in the same grade levels in approximately the same sequence, is absolutely fundamental to developing an articulated, aligned curriculum system. Once this curriculum system standardizes what will be taught and when it will be taught, the system can begin to monitor and improve itself. Without guarantees or even ideas about what is being taught and when it is being taught, a continuous improvement cycle cannot be used. Once the district has standardized the curriculum system, then the Plan, Do, Check, Act cycle can be applied. The system can then look at student performance results to see if this initial design is working or needs to be modified. With the Plan, Do, Check, Act cycle in operation, the Quarterly Instructional Objectives and Power Standards will improve with each iteration.

DEVELOPING THE QUARTERLY INSTRUCTIONAL OBJECTIVES

Depending on when in the school year the Power Standards are deployed, the development of the Quarterly Instructional Objectives will follow accordingly. Some schools use a task force to develop the Power Standards and Quarterly Instructional Objectives during the spring and summer of the year. This greatly reduces substitute issues and is readily accomplished in that time frame. This allows for a beginning-of-the-year rollout of both the Power Standards and the Quarterly Instructional Objectives to the entire staff during the opening of school as well as great discussions and exchanges of ideas during those initial back-to-school meetings and faculty meetings during August and September. Other districts develop both the Power Standards and the Quarterly Instructional Objectives during the summer (my experience shows that this takes about three full days of task force work), again making them ready for distribution at the beginning of the school year.

Remember, this entire process is subject to the Plan, Do, Check, Act cycle, so the Power Standards and Quarterly Instructional Objectives will be distributed, and the feedback forms and processes, including due dates and sharing of results information, will be included in the packets (see Chapter 3 and Resource C). This allows every teacher to try the new approach, provide feedback, and hear back from the task force about decisions/changes.

Some school districts develop only the Power Standards as the first step. They then design the development of the Quarterly Instructional Objectives into the school calendar during the school year. This allows teachers to experiment with Quarterly Instructional Objectives and provide feedback to the task force. The task force then meets during the school year and develops the Quarterly Instructional Objectives on the fly. As the Quarterly Instructional Objectives are developed, it is no longer essential to have the entire task force meet. The third-grade teachers or the third-grade members of the task force can meet during school with subs, after school with extra-duty pay, during school improvement or release-time days, or at other times to do the work of developing Quarterly Instructional Objectives.

The task force, as part of its general meeting that all members attend, will need to use the discussion guide in the Follow-Up Process Guidelines: Instructional Objectives box to develop the specific process and steps that will be followed in this development and feedback process (this, like the other forms presented, is an actual form used in the process). This allows the task force to design the specific process to fit the needs of the local district and to share those decisions with the entire staff. Feel free to use this form or modify it as you see fit.

Again, the software provided by Partners4results (www.partners 4results.org) is especially helpful here in creating, editing, and publishing the Quarterly Instructional Objectives and will house and share those documents with the staff and community.

FOLLOW-UP PROCESS GUIDELINES: INSTRUCTIONAL OBJECTIVES

This group may not answer all of these questions today. We should begin the discussion today and develop a process with dates to ensure this work gets decided on and completed. With time and commitment, this will become part of a yearly cycle that will allow the curriculum to always be under review and continually improved. The first year or so will be a bit more difficult as timelines are set and processes for review and revision are established. Please be patient and help by being part of the solution. Share your ideas and help us continually improve.

The Plan cycle was completed by the work of this group; now we must make sure we follow up with the Do, Check, and Act cycles.

Do Cycle

- When will the Quarterly Instructional Objectives be due?
- To whom?
- In what format? Electronic? On a form?
- What will they look like? Numbering system? 8LA1, 7M2?
- Will the task force see them prior to final publication? When? Meeting called by whom?
- When will they be published and distributed to staff? By whom? Any follow-up activity by the task force as part of the distribution?

Check Cycle

- When will we gather initial feedback about the Power Standards and Quarterly Instructional Objectives?
- Who will gather and collate?
- Will we allow midcourse corrections or stick with the initial product for the first year?
- When will we gather end-of-year feedback? By whom? How?

Act Cycle

- When will we meet to review the feedback and make improvements and corrections?
- When and how will we release this second version (and subsequent versions)?

These Quarterly Instructional Objectives are generally lists of far less than one page per quarter that contain five to ten bulleted skills that all students are expected to know and be able to do within the quarter. These are developed and agreed on through the group work of the task force. This process, like the process of determining Power Standards, can be exciting and at times controversial. As long as the tone remains respectful, such passion and excitement are great. Why wouldn't teachers get passionate about what they believe is most important for students to learn? Why wouldn't professionals be excited about what they believe is best for kids? Such heated conversations, as long as they remain respectful, help everyone frame their own beliefs and feelings while listening to others' ideas.

During the development of the Quarterly Instructional Objectives, teachers will frequently ask to bring in their assigned textbooks to aid in this process of developing Quarterly Instructional Objectives. I ask that they never bring textbooks to this phase of the development. We are designing and sequencing the student learning to reflect the order in which kids can best learn the material to master the Power Standards, not the chapters in the book. On more than one occasion, teachers have protested that the first Quarterly Instructional Objective is contained in, say, Chapter 7 of the book, so how can they possibly begin teaching in Chapter 7 of the book? This is a very important part of the new system. The textbook must match the curriculum, not vice versa.

The original task force, grade-level groups, or course-specific groups will work together as a team to develop common Quarterly Instructional Objectives to guide instruction for the quarter. As a team of professional educators assigned to a specific grade level or course, teachers will develop a set of common specific instructional objectives for each of the four quarters in a school year. What specifically must students know and be able to do, and in what order must these skills be taught and assessed? The Quarterly Instructional Objectives give teachers the direction to plan specific classroom instruction and assessments to help students meet a common Power Standard and to measure students' progress toward that goal in a sequenced, common approach. This is another step in the all-important area of curriculum alignment, that is, aligning what the district teaches to what the state assesses.

As these Quarterly Instructional Objectives are developed, it is critical to make sure all of the subskills used to define reading, math, or whatever subject are contained in the Quarterly Instructional Objectives. For example, if the state defines reading as vocabulary, drawing inference from text, understanding concrete meaning, root words, and so forth, it is critical to cover these subskills in the Quarterly Instructional Objectives.

This will be very important in the development of assessments and using that data to design instruction. Just make sure each subskill is tagged with at least one Quarterly Instructional Objective. This will not only help teachers better understand the assessment system but also ensure balance in the development of the Quarterly Instructional Objectives designed to drive everyday instruction. All the subskills measured by the state will be addressed in classroom instruction. This will also help in the reporting format that will then tie student performance directly to the subskills in the state standards. The Partners4results software automatically ties these Quarterly Instructional Objectives to state standards.

Further, it is critical that during this phase when Quarterly Instructional Objectives are being developed, time be set aside for vertical and horizontal articulation. As grade levels/departments develop their first drafts of Quarterly Instructional Objectives, these need to be shared with other grade levels and courses within the departments. This does two very important things:

1. It shares the objectives with the entire group and helps the group come to consensus about what a Quarterly Instructional Objective is. This clarifies for the entire group what it should be doing and allows the group to exchange ideas and suggestions.

2. It allows for vertical articulation. Third grade or Algebra 1, for example, gets to see exactly the skills the subsequent course will be expecting students to learn. Vertical and horizontal articulation is the essence of this approach, so let's make sure we do it at every juncture.

With this kind of instructional system alignment, the importance of Power Standards to clearly focus instruction cannot be overemphasized. The building/district simply cannot expect such a finely aligned curriculum document to be faithfully implemented if that curriculum document doesn't provide the focus that makes those expected instructional objectives specific enough to be learnable. The building/district cannot take the entire list of state standards, divide those state standards into fourths, and assign one-fourth of the state standards to each quarter—that is too much to teach, much less to learn. Remember, focus, focus, focus.

While the initial work of developing Power Standards and Quarterly Instructional Objectives is demanding and takes time, it pays huge dividends as the year unfolds and in future years to reduce teachers' workload. No longer will planning be subject to chapters in the book or other extraneous factors. Local professionals will have decided on Quarterly Instructional Objectives for each quarter. These Quarterly Instructional Objectives will then be used to develop daily and weekly lesson plans.

Teachers will understand and be able to communicate to parents and students the specific intended learnings for the quarter, and these Power Standards and Quarterly Instructional Objectives will be subject to the continuous improvement strategy of Plan, Do, Check, Act to constantly improve and refine them.

If a controversy develops over a specific Quarterly Instructional Objective, as will likely happen, have teachers come to consensus to try the Quarterly Instructional Objective. If it works, great! If not, it can be improved for the following year through the Plan, Do, Check, Act cycle. That is why every teacher must implement the Quarterly Instructional Objectives as designed. The district cannot study and improve a system that is not doing the same things across grade levels or courses. Without consistency in learner expectations, there is no system, only a loosely configured group creating disparate results based on disparate efforts—all well intentioned but neither coordinated nor aligned.

While I was working with a district, I happened to be in the office when a teacher submitted her first Quarterly Instructional Objectives. I noticed there were fourteen objectives and said something to the effect of, "That's quite a few Quarterly Instructional Objectives." She immediately became defensive and asked me, had I ever taught biology or science, who was I to challenge her, and so forth. I quickly apologized and explained that it was just an observation, not a judgment. A year later, after the teacher taught the Quarterly Instructional Objectives and went through the first year of the Plan, Do, Check, Act cycle, I couldn't help but notice that the number of Quarterly Instructional Objectives for that course was down to seven in the second draft.

SAMPLES AND NUMBERING THE QUARTERLY INSTRUCTIONAL OBJECTIVES

In Chapter 3, the numbering system used with the Power Standards was explained. That numbering system will now be applied and expanded to define the Quarterly Instructional Objectives. The Power Standard 3M refers to the third-grade Math Power Standard. Let's use this numbering process on a sample set of Power Standards and Quarterly Instructional Objectives developed by the staff in Morrison, Illinois. This should give you not only a sample of the Power Standards and Quarterly Instructional Objectives but also a look at some real work done by your colleagues. You should note that there are numbers assigned to each Quarterly Instructional Objective; 3M refers to third-grade math. The first number following 3M refers to the quarter the instructional objective refers to, 1 being first quarter, and so on. The number following the decimal point is the number of the actual Quarterly Instructional Objective. Therefore, Quarterly Instructional Objective 3M1.3 refers to the Quarterly Instructional Objective in third-grade math, first quarter, third instructional objective. Further examples of Quarterly Instructional Objectives are available at www.partners4results.org/demo.

Developed by the teachers and administrators in Morrison, Illinois, the third-grade Power Standards and Quarterly Instructional Objectives shown in the Third-Grade Math Power Standard: 3M box demonstrate the concept well. These Quarterly Instructional Objectives are based, of course, on the Illinois learning standards, the Illinois Standards Achievement Test, and the judgment of the teachers and administrators about what they believe all kids must know and be able to do. It should also be noted that on the 2006 Illinois Standards Achievement Test, 99 percent of Morrison third graders met or exceeded the Illinois standards in math, so the district has surely demonstrated competence in instruction and alignment.

THIRD-GRADE MATH POWER STANDARD: 3M

By the end of third grade, the student will be able to

- use counting comparison, estimation, and numeric relationships in whole and fractional numbers;
- demonstrate a knowledge of basic addition, subtraction, and multiplication facts;
- solve one-step problems using multiple-digit addition and subtraction and single-digit multiplication problem–solving strategies;
- use appropriate techniques to determine units of measurement, money, and time; and
- identify geometric shapes.

Third-Grade Math Instructional Objectives, First Quarter

The student will

- 3M1.1—demonstrate basic knowledge of addition facts from 0 to 18;
- 3M1.2—count by 2s, 5s, 10s, and 100s;
- 3M1.3—identify place value of ones and tens;
- 3M1.4—identify a square, rectangle, circle, triangle, trapezoid, polygon, and parallelogram;
- 3M1.5—measure to the nearest inch and centimeter;
- 3M1.6—solve one-step multiple-digit addition problems;
- 3M1.7—count by pennies, nickels, and dimes;
- 3M1.8—tell time to the nearest hour and half hour; and
- 3M1.9—draw and read a bar graph.

Third-Grade Math Instructional Objectives, Second Quarter

The student will

- 3M2.1—demonstrate basic knowledge of subtraction facts from 0 to 10;
- 3M2.2—count by 7s, 25s, and 3s;
- 3M2.3—identify place value of hundreds;
- 3M2.4—identify a hexagon, octagon, and pentagon;
- 3M2.5—add two-digit numbers using the addition algorithm;
- 3M2.6—round and estimate to the nearest 10;
- 3M2.7—solve one-step multiple-digit subtraction problems;
- 3M2.8—measure to the nearest half inch;
- 3M2.9—count by quarters;
- 3M2.10—tell time to the nearest quarter hour;
- 3M2.11—tell elapsed time to the nearest hour and half hour; and
- 3M2.12—draw and read a pictograph and tally chart.

Third-Grade Math Instructional Objectives, Third Quarter

The student will

- 3M3.1—demonstrate subtraction facts from 10 to 18;
- 3M3.2—count by 4s and ½s;
- 3M3.3—identify place value of thousands;
- 3M3.4—identify a rhombus (diamond, parallelogram);
- 3M3.5—compare the order of fractions—¼, ½, and ⅓;
- 3M3.6—subtract two-digit numbers;
- 3M3.7—add three-digit numbers;
- 3M3.8—round and estimate to the nearest hundred;
- 3M3.9—solve one-step single-digit multiplication problems;
- 3M3.10—add money amounts;
- 3M3.11—tell time to the nearest minute; and
- 3M3.12—identify ordinal positions.

Third-Grade Math Instructional Objectives, Fourth Quarter

The student will

- 3M4.1—demonstrate basic knowledge of multiplication facts from 0 to 9;
- 3M4.2—count by 9s, 6s, ¼s, and 8s;
- 3M4.3—add and subtract fractions with like denominators;
- 3M4.4—subtract three-digit numbers;
- 3M4.5—measure to the nearest tenth of a centimeter;
- 3M4.6—measure to the nearest quarter inch; and
- 3M4.7—identify perpendicular lines and line segments.

These Quarterly Instructional Objectives are the result of the work process previously described; that is, the teachers went through the entire process outlined in the Third-Grade Math Power Standard: 3M box and came to consensus on these Quarterly Instructional Objectives. These specific Quarterly Instructional Objectives are the first draft of Morrison's Quarterly Instructional Objectives and will, of course, be subject to the Plan, Do, Check, Act cycle of continuous improvement. However, it is worth taking the time to look at Morrison's Quarterly Instructional Objectives and understanding the logical flow of instruction these teachers and administrators are trying to create. This is the same kind of work you will want to emulate in designing your own Quarterly Instructional Objectives, based, of course, on your own state standards and resulting Power Standards.

> We have met the enemy, and he is us.
>
> —Pogo

Let's review how these Power Standards and Quarterly Instructional Objectives work. If it looks like this (Power Standard) at the end of the year, what will teachers have to teach (Quarterly Instructional Objectives) first quarter? Second quarter? Third quarter? Fourth quarter? A logical progression of skills moves from quarter to quarter in an order that educators believe will maximize student learning. Are the Quarterly Instructional Objectives in the Third-Grade Math Power Standard: 3M box perfect? Probably not. Do they give teachers the instructional focus to know exactly what they are expected to teach and students are expected to learn for each quarter? Yes, and these Quarterly Instructional Objectives will improve as they go through the continuous improvement loop.

The most critical issue here is that the Morrison staff, as a group of professional educators, followed the national research and came to consensus on what third-grade children must know and be able to do in math in Morrison, Illinois. This gives the teachers the instructional focus to produce focused, aligned learning. Returning as well as new teachers in Morrison, Illinois, are given these specific curriculum documents, which clearly and succinctly define the intended learning for the year in a quarter-by-quarter format. The same curriculum articulation is happening in Morrison at every grade level and in every subject. The curriculum is aligned, both horizontally and vertically, and it is aligned to the Illinois state standards.

Further, a teacher can look at the same documents for the grade level preceding the grade level he or she teaches and see very specifically what students were expected to learn the previous year. That teacher can look ahead and see exactly what his or her students will be expected to know and be able to do in the following year. Curriculum alignment, and therefore student attainment of that curriculum, is no longer a matter of chance or teacher assignment but rather the result of specific planning and choices made and implemented by educational professionals who agreed on what all students must know and be able to do.

Used by the Morrison staff and other schools and districts, the process described in this book has created ownership and a sense of educational accomplishment. Staff and administration have worked together to make this happen in all grades and classes, and they are already seeing the results of their combined efforts.

Let's get back to the numbering system for a bit. This numbering system is exceptionally important in building this instructional system. In this example, the third-grade teachers in Morrison, Illinois, have agreed that these are the skills that students must learn by quarters of the academic year. As a teacher designs a lesson on 3M1.3, the specific skill to be taught is evident. The focus of the lesson is equally clear. Which part of the textbook, if any, will be used in teaching this lesson to master this Quarterly Instructional Objective? The backward design of a standards-based lesson can now be used.

The Partners4results software package allows for the electronic creation, storage, and scoring of all assessments used. Once a quiz or test is developed, it can be stored on the system for use by other teachers or for use the following year.

As multiple teachers develop lessons around 3M1.3, assessments and instructional materials can be shared and improved. Since all teachers in a grade level will be covering the same Quarterly Instructional Objectives during the same quarter, such sharing will be greatly enhanced. Teachers will now be able to share student progress on Quarterly Instructional Objectives and discuss why some approaches work better than others. Regrouping to address student learning issues can now go across classrooms as teachers teaching the same Quarterly Instructional Objectives share information about students' learning or failing to learn a specific Quarterly Instructional Objective. This system can do much to reduce the isolation of the classroom teacher and to help teachers share resources and strategies.

REALITIES OF THE QUARTERLY INSTRUCTIONAL OBJECTIVES

This consistency in instructional focus allows for much more common planning and resource sharing as all teachers, students, and parents know the specific instructional focus for the quarter. Lessons and assessments developed to measure these very specific skills can be shared across classrooms and improved through feedback.

Districts can now adopt new textbooks based on how closely the proposed texts align to the district's curriculum (Power Standards and Quarterly Instructional Objectives) rather than order a new textbook and then revamp the math program to fit the new book. It will now become a case of the curriculum expectations' driving the selection of the textbook rather than vice versa.

Since all teachers will be held accountable for teaching this very specific set of Quarterly Instructional Objectives in a specific quarter of the year, conversations across grade levels and individual courses can readily focus on the very specific list of Quarterly Instructional Objectives teachers will all be teaching and how to best teach and assess those Quarterly Instructional Objectives. In the traditional, unaligned system, the creation of common assessments has been stymied by the fact that every teacher has taught different content and skills during the same time frame. Sometimes these instructional or content differences are small, but usually the differences in material and content are so great that any kind of common assessment or comparison is impossible. The proposed numbering system will greatly expedite such common planning and assessments.

Think back to the example in Chapter 1 wherein all of the biology teachers defined biology differently; those teachers could not have shared instruction or assessment strategies since they were teaching significantly different content in the same course. By creating Quarterly Instructional Objectives that base instruction on skills rather than content, the system improves the opportunity for teachers to share assessments and instructional strategies. If a teacher experiences incredible success with a particular Quarterly Instructional Objective in a specific quarter, why not share the strategies and assessments used with the teacher across the hall? Why develop instructional strategies or assessments individually when the teacher across the hall has already done that work?

It must also be said that the district "owns" the course and grants credit for its successful completion. When teachers say, "That's not what I teach in Algebra I" (or any other subject), I think it is important to remind them that the school/district is responsible for the course and issuance of the credit, not the teacher. The district has every right, and I believe obligation, to determine what the course content will be. These errors are generally errors of passion—teachers usually love what they teach and, for years, have been granted unlimited freedom to decide what to teach. Be patient and help them understand the importance and mutual benefit of coming to consensus on what students must learn. Life for everyone will be easier when the system defines and enforces expected learnings, but not instructional strategies used. Remember, this effort is about defining what is learned, not how it is taught.

PUBLISHING AND REVIEWING THE QUARTERLY INSTRUCTIONAL OBJECTIVES

Many of the publishing issues discussed earlier in this chapter (see Publishing and Communication Issues) about Power Standards apply to the publishing of Quarterly Instructional Objectives. That is, they should be published by one central location that has shown a flair for such work and then distributed, in both hard copy and electronic formats, to buildings and teachers who will communicate these very specific academic expectations to members of the educational community. Again, software to do this publishing and Internet hosting is available and demonstrated at www.partners4results.org/demo.

As a communication tool to students and parents, these Quarterly Instructional Objectives are invaluable. Teachers can post these quarterly expectations in the classroom and send them home in newsletters. Teachers will also use them as the basis for developing daily lesson plans. By referencing all classroom learning to the Quarterly Instructional Objectives, students are able to better understand the expectations. Remember the huge gains in student performance that are reported when students know in advance of the instruction the skills they are expected to know.

These Quarterly Instructional Objectives, like the Power Standards, also can be enlarged and posted in the classroom, serving as excellent focal points for students in understanding academic expectations. When given to parents, these Quarterly Instructional Objectives describe what is going on in the classroom. While a parent may not be sure of what *number sense* means in the kindergarten state math standards, the Quarterly Instructional Objective of counting groups of objects to ten helps a parent understand what his or her child must know and be able to do. These Quarterly Instructional Objectives can truly engage parents and students in the educational process.

Like the Power Standards and all this curriculum and assessment work, the Quarterly Instructional Objectives will be subject to the Plan, Do, Check, Act cycle to ensure continuous improvement in student learning. Teachers provide and process feedback, which when coupled with decision-making responsibility and accountability, gives them a dominant voice in the reform of curriculum and instruction. This is exactly what must happen for real, systemic change to occur and last. Public education must empower local educators to control and refine the curriculum to best reflect the state standards and state assessments. Judging the effectiveness of educational reform by the quality and scope of improved student performance frames the reform initiative in the most important context—improved student learning.

Sample documents and forms shown in Resource C and in the Initial Distribution Feedback box will help the reader better understand the continuous improvement process and how to implement it in a reform initiative. Remember, this entire process is built on teacher involvement and allowing teachers to make decisions based on national research, what's best for kids, and data. The system must deliberately and regularly seek feedback from teachers on how the Power Standards and Quarterly Instructional Objectives are working and get their input to see if these curriculum documents are working as intended. This review and revision work can easily be done by the task force that did the initial development work and, in my experience, usually takes less than a day of work.

But such a yearly review/revision cycle is absolutely critical if the Power Standards and Quarterly Instructional Objectives are to remain viable documents and not end up on a shelf gathering dust.

In the Initial Distribution Feedback box is one of the forms used to gather such feedback. Please note this form seeks feedback on both the Power Standards and the Quarterly Instructional Objectives. Using this form, or one very similar to it, on a regular basis ensures the Plan, Do, Check, Act cycle is consistently employed. As your work with these issues continues and improves, the forms will be adapted accordingly. As with the other forms, spaces have been deleted for ease of publishing.

INITIAL DISTRIBUTION FEEDBACK

1 is bad; 5 is good.

1. I understand the Power Standards and Quarterly Instructional Objectives.

1	2	3	4	5
Strongly Disagree	Disagree	Neutral	Agree	Strongly Agree

Comments (use back of page if needed):

2. I understand what I am expected to do with the new Power Standards and Quarterly Instructional Objectives.

1	2	3	4	5
Strongly Disagree	Disagree	Neutral	Agree	Strongly Agree

Comments (use back of page if needed):

3. I believe I am capable of teaching the Power Standards and Quarterly Instructional Objectives.

1	2	3	4	5
Strongly Disagree	Disagree	Neutral	Agree	Strongly Agree

Comments (use back of page if needed):

4. I believe our students are capable of learning these Power Standards and Quarterly Instructional Objectives in the grade level to which these standards are assigned.

1	2	3	4	5
Strongly Disagree	Disagree	Neutral	Agree	Strongly Agree

Comments (use back of page if needed):

5. I would be willing to volunteer to work with the Power Standards task force to continue and improve this work.

1	2	3	4	5
Strongly Disagree	Disagree	Neutral	Agree	Strongly Agree

Comments (use back of page if needed):

Grade Level: _____ Building: _____

Signature (Optional): _____

Make sure to build the continuous improvement loop into the follow-up process, which includes a yearly review of Power Standards, Quarterly Instructional Objectives, student performance data, and teacher feedback. Continuous improvement must be deliberately and intentionally designed into the implementation process to make sure that data drive improvement initiatives, allowing true systemic reform to occur. Remember, you developed these Power Standards and Quarterly Instructional Objectives to improve student performance. Make sure to look at your student performance data as a gauge of the effectiveness of the Power Standards and Quarterly Instructional Objectives. These Power Standards and Quarterly Instructional Objectives should be "tuned up" to continuously improve student performance. If they are truly aligned to the state standards and assessments, they should result in improvements in student performance, and they will, provided you ensure they are used by every teacher.

The usual pattern for this annual review/revision work is to distribute the feedback sheets to the teachers in the late spring or include the feedback sheets as part of the packet of materials distributed at the beginning of the year. Spring distribution, while not always popular because of the press of things to be done during the last month of school, can happen during May so the review sheets can get to task force members before the end of the school year.

An alternative that worked well was to make the curriculum feedback sheets part of the end-of-year checkout package that teachers complete before school ends. The feedback sheets were then hand-gathered by building principals (to encourage the return of as many feedback sheets as possible) and forwarded to task forces within a week of the close of school so the task force could meet right after school was out and before everyone scattered for the summer. This method also gives building principals very specific feedback on the project's status in their buildings—feedback that can be essential in the continuous improvement process. This also allows task forces to finalize all revisions and turn them in before July 1 so that publication and distribution of the revised materials can be part of the teachers' welcome-back packet in August.

You now have the knowledge and processes to create Power Standards and Quarterly Instructional Objectives for every grade level and course taught in the building/district. These documents have the ability to align the curriculum in the building/district to the state standards and to significantly improve student learning and performance. This is the reason we, as educators, chose teaching as our life's work—to improve the lives and learning of students.

PROCESS SUMMARY

The initial work of the task force is completed, and now you have to distribute that work, gather feedback, and make sure that work gets implemented appropriately. Further, you will now provide the leadership to take the group to the next level, the Quarterly Instructional Objectives. The group should be functioning well by now, and communication and process issues should be resolved, so just keep the group moving at this point. The development of the Quarterly Instructional Objectives will be very similar in process to the development of the Power Standards, and the articulation and deployment issues are similar as well.

Political Issues

During this phase, political concerns should no longer be paramount. You addressed these early in the project, so your major responsibility is to keep everyone informed and comfortable with the project and where it is going and make sure nobody tries to "kidnap" or dominate the process. Address any concerns quickly and honestly.

Leadership Issues

The major leadership skills will be group facilitation and listening to the group in the development of timelines for developing the Quarterly Instructional Objectives. There must be a mix of expediency to get the job done and caution to make sure it gets done right. Take your time and listen to concerns. Also, Board of Education adoption of the Power Standards and Quarterly Instructional Objectives, if decided on, will require leadership. The use of these documents by the entire district as the required curriculum documents for planning instruction will require leadership at both the central office and building levels.

Continuous Improvement Issues

As the second major phase of the project is completed, the continuous improvement processes must be present in every step. The deliberate solicitation of the district staff for feedback, the processing of that feedback by the task force, and the reporting back to the district staff about decisions will be seriously addressed from this point forward. Remember, Plan, Do, Check, Act never ends—we are in this for the long haul to ensure continuous improvement. This deliberate addressing of the Plan, Do, Check, Act cycle will be closely monitored by your critics and speak volumes to the entire staff about the true reforms being implemented.

Technical Skills

During this phase of the project, the Power Standards are being deployed and published, and the Quarterly Instructional Objectives are being developed. There is not such a defined linear progression as in the initial development of Power Standards.

PROCESS CHECKLIST

Make sure you do or consider the following:

- ❏ Review goals, roles, and responsibilities with the task force.
- ❏ Publish the final set of Power Standards as an impeccable document that is distributed both in hard copy and electronically to all members of the educational community.
- ❏ Decide whether you will have the Board of Education officially adopt the Power Standards as the curriculum document for the building/district.

(Continued)

(Continued)

☐ Remember, use of the Power Standards and Quarterly Instructional Objectives cannot be an option—make sure everyone is using them.

☐ Provide a forum for exchange of publication/communication strategies with the Power Standards and Quarterly Instructional Objectives among the various buildings and so forth. Let everyone learn from others' work and ideas by sharing effective communication techniques about the Power Standards.

☐ Decide on the timing of the development of the Quarterly Instructional Objectives. This will depend on the time of the school year and the comfort of the district with the process. This work can be done over the summer or during the school year. Plans will be driven by local situations and realities.

☐ Make sure everyone knows the Quarterly Instructional Objectives are based on the Power Standards and represent a logical flow in the instruction of children. Teachers are trying to define not only what is learned but when it is learned and in what order.

☐ The group that develops the Quarterly Instructional Objectives may or may not be the same group that developed the Power Standards. Leadership must make that decision.

☐ Make sure the subskills used by the state to define a content area such as math (geometric thinking, algebraic reasoning, number sense, etc.) are reflected in and tagged to the Quarterly Instructional Objectives.

☐ The numbering system for the Quarterly Instructional Objectives is critical to their successful deployment. Remember, this is about creating an instructional system. This will be especially important in both the instruction phase and the assessment phase of the project.

☐ Make sure the number of Quarterly Instructional Objectives represents both a learnable and an assessable amount of curriculum—remember a learnable curriculum: don't teach your dog to whistle.

☐ Ensure time is set aside to vertically articulate the objectives across grade levels and courses.

☐ Ensure the Quarterly Instructional Objectives differentiate between the need to know and the nice to know.

☐ The feedback and continuous improvement process for the Quarterly Instructional Objectives, like the Power Standards, must be built into the process from the beginning.

☐ The deployment of the Quarterly Instructional Objectives, like the Power Standards, cannot be an option. It must be faithfully deployed by everyone in the system. Remember, DWYSYWD!

5

Planning for Common, Aligned Assessments

CHAPTER EXPECTATIONS

This chapter explains the concept of aligned assessments and presents a process to create those common, aligned assessments. This chapter is not intended to evaluate or explain the various types of classroom assessments used by classroom teachers on a daily basis but rather to describe a process that can be used to develop local common, aligned assessments that are administered in all grade levels at a prescribed time and are aligned to the state standards, Power Standards, and Quarterly Instructional Objectives. These common, aligned assessments are sometimes called benchmark assessments. The chapter will close with an explanation of scoring these assessments and how, by using this new system, much more specific data can be created to facilitate the data-feedback loop to improve student performance.

WHAT ARE COMMON, ALIGNED ASSESSMENTS?

A brief explanation is in order to help the reader understand the issues involved in developing assessments. State assessments are designed to be summative assessments. Like the final exams given at the end of specific courses, the state summative assessments are intended to measure what students have learned. As Larry Lezotte frequently points out, these scores are trailing indicators of student performance as they happen after the fact and cannot affect the measured learning anymore. Because they are given after the instruction to see how much was learned, these state summative assessments are much like getting on the scale in the doctor's office at the end of a six-week diet—how much weight was lost or gained? Now that the patient is on the scale, there is no sense worrying about the diet anymore. The meals that should not have been eaten or the exercises that should have been done are now over—this is the final summative evaluation of the patient's efforts.

> Doug Reeves notes that the purpose of assessments is the improvement of student performance.

The other kind of assessment used in education is the formative assessment, or the assessment given along the way to see how the learning is going and what midcourse adjustments need to be made. Rick Stiggins frequently calls them "assessments for learning." Teachers should give these assessments to judge how the students are learning and should use the results to adjust the instruction accordingly. Again, like the trips to the scale the patient makes during the diet, before going to the doctor for the final weigh-in, formative assessments ask, How is the student/patient doing? Does he or she need to make changes before that final weigh-in? However, in the current system, most formative assessments are given to determine grades and assess whether the student learned Chapter 4, the content of a novel, or whatever.

> One of the questions Lezotte is frequently asked is, "How often do you assess kids?" He always replies, "How prepared are you to alter instruction?" If you are not prepared to alter instruction, why bother to assess?

WHY USE COMMON ASSESSMENTS?

While educators can use the results of the state assessment to make some curricular decisions, the once-a-year test does not give us the kind of frequent, ongoing information needed to make regular instructional decisions leading to improved instruction and, therefore, learning. Using the yearly state assessment scores as the only measure of the curriculum and student learning is like going on a diet and weighing in once a year. While the yearly weight is a data point, it is far too infrequent to plan and implement intervention and/or instructional strategies.

> As Doug Reeves says, the cardinal principle of measurement is that it is more important and accurate to measure a few things frequently and consistently than to measure many things once.

What is being proposed in this chapter, along with much of the national research, is a set of common, quarterly (formative) assessments given to all students in a grade level or course to ensure those students are making progress toward the state summative assessment, ACT, SAT, or whatever summative, end-of-year assessment is used in that state. In the overall curriculum alignment process advocated in this book, the hardest work has been done. Through the use of district personnel, Power Standards aligned to the state standards have been created and agreed to by the entire staff. In the second phase of this project, the Quarterly Instructional Objectives were created, again aligned to the state standards through the Power Standards. Now begins the work of developing the common, aligned assessments to measure student progress toward the Power Standards.

This use of the common, formative quarterly assessments does several things for the local building/district. It gives quarterly (and sometimes more frequent) reports about student progress toward meeting the state goals for learning as evidenced in the state assessment. This allows teachers to evaluate progress, make midcourse adjustments to instruction, and address specific, diagnosed weaknesses in student learning. As a result, teachers use the assessments *for* learning, as Rick Stiggins teaches us, rather than as assessments *of* learning.

To review, by using the numbering system advocated in this book for Quarterly Instructional Objectives, data are automatically separated into subskills within an academic area. By applying the numbering system explained in Chapter 4 to the development of these common, aligned assessments, you will be able to get much more informative data—data that can greatly enhance regrouping, acceleration, and other instructional decisions. That is, you will know not only the students' overall score on the assessment but also which particular subskills (algebraic reasoning, vocabulary, or whatever) each student is strong in or needs help with. This will be explained in greater detail later in the chapter.

Also, especially at the secondary level, these common, aligned assessments guarantee that the content of all Algebra I classes, and other classes for that matter, is similar and that the same academic standard has been applied in all classes that share a common course title. Think back to the biology example in Chapter 1; there was no way the students in the various biology classes were being exposed to the same curriculum or academic standards. This curriculum system helps align instruction across grade levels and courses and makes sure that the curriculum commitments that were made in developing Power Standards and Quarterly Instructional Objectives are followed. Also, the Plan, Do, Check, Act cycle will be applied to determine whether student performance is improving as expected and whether adjustments to the Power Standards, the Quarterly Instructional Objectives, or instruction are needed.

Further, once the common, aligned assessments are designed, the need for individually generated teacher assessments is greatly reduced.

All teachers know what the midsemester test and final semester exam will be, so the creation of individual midterm or final assessments is not necessary. Groups of teachers can work together (in professional learning communities?) to develop these assessments and discuss the critical learnings and the way students will demonstrate those learnings. The isolation of the classroom teacher is significantly reduced as groups of professionals work together to determine and standardize assessment practices.

And don't forget, these common, aligned assessments, like everything created through this process, will go through the Plan, Do, Check, Act cycle to continuously improve. If teachers disagree on any specific aspects of these assessments, it is logical to try whichever approach seems most appropriate or politically expedient. Yes, sometimes political expediency enters into curricular decisions. If a decision threatens to alienate people and destroy support for the process, then trying the approach to see if it works is acceptable. If it works, great! If it doesn't work, the system will try another way. As I have said before, God bless Plan, Do, Check, Act. Try it, see if it works, then decide.

Remember, this is now a standards-based environment. Of greatest importance is that all students learn the standard, not just those who learn the standard the fastest or the easiest. This requires an entirely new teaching cycle. Educators can no longer teach, test, and move on. In this new instructional process mandated by state standards, they teach the standard, assess student learning, then use that assessment data to redesign instruction and reteach the standard to enhance student mastery. By limiting the standards to be taught through Power Standards and limiting the quarterly instructional focus through Quarterly Instructional Objectives, teachers now have the time to focus on teaching, assessing, and reteaching.

This revolutionizes education because this approach signifies a quantum change from the way educators have done business for many years. Teachers have assigned grades based on how quickly students learn the material and, unfortunately, left behind those who struggle. Again, it is important to reiterate that teachers taught this way because that was how the system was designed, with education as the great sorter and separator of American society. Teachers were not evil people trying to deny learning to students; they were following the rules of the system in place. In this new curricular approach, the system limits the number of standards to the important few and designs instruction around those important standards. As this is a new approach for almost everyone on the staff, leadership must provide the needed staff development and take the time to allow the new grading/teaching paradigm to sink in. Do not force the issue and endanger the entire project—provide the needed staff development and the time to internalize and operationalize these new learnings.

Since the Quarterly Instructional Objectives give incredibly specific direction to the teachers regarding expectations for student learning, local personnel can develop the common, aligned assessments. The Quarterly

Instructional Objectives have been definitively stated, so the creation of the assessments to measure the specific Quarterly Instructional Objectives is much simpler now. Remember, the Quarterly Instructional Objectives are designed to represent a learnable amount of curriculum. We cannot expect students to learn forty-four instructional objectives per quarter to ensure we cover the entire book. We have taken steps to ensure a learnable amount of curriculum; now it is time to design appropriate assessments. Look back at the sample Quarterly Instructional Objectives in Chapter 4; wouldn't development of assessments for those be relatively doable by local teachers?

It is also important to consider the timing of the development of these common, aligned assessments, the next phase of this initiative. As discussed earlier, the Power Standards are done in the first year, while the Quarterly Instructional Objectives are done in the first and/or second year of the project, depending on the timing, resources, and inclination of the building/district. The development of the common, aligned assessments will definitely be further on down the line, after the building/district is confident that the Power Standards and Quarterly Instructional Objectives are appropriate and working as intended.

Some districts deploy the Power Standards and Quarterly Instructional Objectives the first semester, then spend the second semester developing common assessments. The initial common assessments are developed and piloted by those teachers who are really excited about the project and willing to move forward (sometimes called the "jumpers") and learn on the fly. This is great, and districts should encourage and support such efforts; they give you your own little innovation incubator where teachers can work together and try to move forward and learn while trying new approaches. This also gives the district time to work out some of the bugs with this pilot group.

While teachers are using the Power Standards and Quarterly Instructional Objectives, some individual teacher experimentation in assessments is bound to occur, and that is also a good thing. Allow and even encourage such experimentation and discuss the efforts and results openly with the entire faculty. This is where the curriculum initiative is going, so why not allow those who want to try new things the freedom and support to do so? Again, what better opportunity is there to be a learning community?

STEPPING OUT OF THE BOX

By following the processes used to develop the Power Standards and Quarterly Instructional Objectives, you have probably noticed several things, but just in case, let's focus on some salient features of this approach that I have observed over the years and that are very important in setting this approach apart from most other initiatives.

1. Based on lots of national research done by Doug Reeves, Larry Lezotte, Mike Schmoker, Rick Stiggins, and others, the reform initiative works. The trick to getting results is following the research faithfully during local implementation. Do it just like the researchers describe it—no shortcuts.

2. The practices in this book are steeped in the correlates of total quality management and continuous improvement, which are, in reality, the business application of the effective schools process. The use of these practices is key to the success of this or any major change initiative.

3. The actual work in this change process is done by the teachers with the support of district personnel. Some districts choose to use outside consultants to provide support. Using local people to conduct the primary work creates local ownership of the finished product and enables local personnel to learn from the process. They develop a much better understanding of state standards and internalize the resulting Power Standards and Quarterly Instructional Objectives, which builds a foundation for continuous improvement and buy-in on future initiatives. Also, local involvement and empowerment increase local competence to stimulate long-term implementation and success.

4. This is all about systemic change, which is the only real kind of lasting change, not a new program or initiative.

Now comes the big difference: while many school districts frequently use district personnel to complete curriculum tasks, the use of local staff, primarily the teachers, to complete the assessment piece is rarely done. However, in this process, due to the specificity of the Quarterly Instructional Objectives and, most important, the numbering system used in them, local teachers can work together to design the quarterly common, aligned assessments as well.

PREDESIGN ISSUES

Before getting into specific design issues, the local teachers must come to understand exactly how the state assessment system assesses local students. For many very good reasons, teachers are committed to the sanctity and confidentiality of the state assessment and, for that matter, all assessments. Teachers don't want to be accused of cheating or taking unfair advantage, but in many cases their commitment to avoiding any contact with state and national assessments has resulted in a poor understanding of how those state and national assessments measure student learning. The system's failure to appropriately train staff leads to an inability to effectively prepare students for those very important assessments. In the many buildings/districts in which I have worked, it never ceases to amaze me how little, if anything, local teachers have been taught about the state or national assessments their students take. This is the perfect opportunity to address this problem in a productive, proactive manner.

This predesign work to help teachers, especially task force members, understand the state assessment system to align their own assessments is best done by the entire task force charged with doing the assessment development. This ensures everyone is given the same information and allowed to process that information as a task force. Once the predesign work is done, the individual grade levels or courses may meet separately to do their work.

> When I was working with a high school on this process, I administered a released copy of the ACT to the entire staff as part of the inservice. Following some initial joking and disbelief, they soon settled into their task. Within twenty minutes, I had open insurrection on my hands. "We don't teach this stuff." "Why would my kids need to know this?" "This isn't part of the science/math/whatever curriculum." And so on it went. Not a single person in the crowd had ever seriously looked at, much less studied, the ACT to see what was on it. Yet the ACT is seen by many as the most important, most meaningful test the students will take during their school careers. In this age of No Child Left Behind, the ACT is even used in some states to judge a school's effectiveness, yet nobody had even bothered to look at it, not even in its released form.
>
> No disrespect is intended; as a matter of fact, this high school staff is incredibly dedicated and has proven a commitment to students in all kinds of ways. But in the old paradigm of education, teachers taught their subject (English, chemistry, whatever), and students learned it or they didn't—the bell curve determined learning. To look at the test was perceived as some kind of scurrilous activity.

It is rare indeed to meet a teacher who has gone to the state website to see which kinds of help are available there. A mystique and belief surrounds testing that gives it a kind of "magical mystery tour" status with educators. Some believe that efforts to understand and use the assessment to prepare students are somehow illegal, or at least unethical. I am not advocating cheating of any kind—that *is* unethical and reprehensible—but to use legitimate, available means to understand and interpret state and/or national assessments to better prepare students is, I believe, a moral and professional obligation.

We must, as professional learning communities, provide the opportunity, resources, and support for teachers to look at, dissect, and study the state assessment system. Each state has information available on its state website about the state assessment system, but please do not for a minute believe many individual teachers take the time and energy to explore it; nor should they. The local educational system needs to lead this all-important initiative. The local educational system does not want, or at least should not want, individual teachers doing all the curriculum and assessment work and making decisions in isolation. However, the district should facilitate such curriculum and assessment work with all the teachers in the system to make sure such work happens. By leading this assessment initiative, the local educational system ensures that all members of the learning community will better understand the assessment system and can help students succeed on those assessments. As mentioned earlier, involving local staff will cultivate local ownership and expertise, which will benefit the building/district for years to come. It is this kind of local ownership and expertise that can lead to true systemic change.

As Lisa Carter (2007) points out in *Total Instructional Alignment*, the alignment of the instruction and assessment to the state standards and the format of the state assessment is critical to improving student performance. That is, we must address not only the alignment of content (e.g., earth science at a specific grade level) but also the contextual alignment (designing instruction and assessments at the same level of Bloom's Taxonomy) to the state assessments. It does little good to align the content of instruction and local assessments to the state's assessment if students are assessed locally only at the knowledge level whereas they are assessed by the state at the higher levels of Bloom. But for local educators to know and apply this assessment knowledge, they must be given the time and leadership to explore and understand the state assessment system and how students are assessed. Please refer to the discussion of the verbs and nouns used in state standards and developing Power Standards—this ensures contextual alignment if the assessments are developed at the same level of Bloom's Taxonomy.

To create this understanding of the state assessment system, someone must accept the leadership role in this process. This should be a local person, preferably the Project Owner, to increase local ownership and expertise. Studying the state assessment system can be done in a day or two by exploring the state website, networking with others around the state, or contacting the state agency. Various states call the assessment documents different things, and whether the state refers to these documents as "blueprints," "released items," "assessment frameworks," or another name, a local person must find, assemble, and interpret all the assessment documents that explain and define the state's assessment system so this information can be shared with the teachers as part of this predesign process.

As the state's assessment system is studied, several important issues or data points must be used and understood in local assessment work. As discussed in the sections about Power Standards and Quarterly Instructional Objectives, every state defines reading, math, and every other content area through various specific subskills or component parts. Reading, for example, has several subskills or component parts that vary from state to state.

Vocabulary may account for 24 percent of the state assessment in one state and as little as 10 percent in another state. That is important information for the design of local assessments, just like it was in the design of Power Standards and Quarterly Instructional Objectives. What other subskills or component skills are used in the state's definition of reading, and in what proportion are they included in the state assessment? These are important issues if those local assessments are to mirror the state assessments.

It is also important to consider how many departments and/or courses within the building/district will be included in the development of the common, aligned assessments. Will driver's education be required to fulfill this obligation? What about wood shop? Band? These are local decisions that each building/district must answer on its own. If you exclude the noncore (frequently called the encore) courses from the process, you run the risk of sending the message that their work is not critical to the building/district mission. If these courses are not critical to the building/district mission, then why even include those courses in the current program of study? Also, in many states, the encore courses do not have state standards or the kinds of state-level documents used to develop the Power Standards and other curriculum documents.

The reality here is that this entire initiative is about coming to consensus as a professional learning community on what the educational system agrees all children must know and be able to do. That being said, why would you offer any course in an academic program that is not important enough to warrant coming to decisions about what we want all kids to know and be able to do and how they must demonstrate that knowledge? If the assessments for an encore course are truly performance based, then the appropriate formative and summative assessments may be performances and not include paper-and-pencil assessments at all. The issue remains that the educational community must come to consensus on what its students must know and be able to do. Allow this discussion to work its way through the educational community and come to a decision that works for the system.

CONSIDERING ASSESSMENT OPTIONS

Let's look at the resources and approaches available and used by some buildings/districts.

1. *Purchasing Ready-Made Tests.* Ready-made tests are available in all kinds of formats: electronic, hard copy, test booklets, and so forth. As mentioned in the discussion about textbook alignment in Chapter 4, finding a set of tests that is exactly aligned to a specific state's standards and/or common core standards is difficult, if not impossible. If they were designed to match only one state's standards, that

would make those tests saleable in only one state. Additionally, remember that you are designing assessments based on Quarterly Instructional Objectives—what the skill must look like at the end of first quarter, not what it looks like on the state assessment. Some of the newer assessment systems are quite good but can be pricey. Using these premade, standardized tests ensures you will be testing curriculum that has not been taught by your teachers—fundamentally unfair to teachers and students.

2. *Purchasing Test-Prep Materials.* These drill-and-kill test prep materials are the stuff of nightmares. When schools go into the three-week test-prep cycle, instruction stops while endless practice tests are given. The result is that kids and teachers justifiably hate the state test. Education can do so much better.

3. *End-of-Chapter Tests From the Textbooks.* The problem here is that the curriculum and assessments your teachers are now using in this system are no longer merely aligned to the textbook. Through Power Standards and Quarterly Instructional Objectives, specific standards and instructional objectives now guide instruction. To use the published end-of-chapter tests in their entirety is to go back on the commitment to align instruction exclusively to the state standards. However, using certain items from these textbook tests that are perfectly aligned to specific Quarterly Instructional Objectives is acceptable and eases the workload of assessment development.

4. *Totally Teacher-Constructed Tests.* The major issue here is that teachers are not psychometrists; that is, they are not trained in developing tests. Relying totally on their skills, with no outside resources, can be frustrating to them and can torpedo the project. Additionally, the finesse and publishing capabilities to produce test items with the multiple-choice format and required mathematical symbols, drawings, and formulas exceed most teachers' technology expertise. Computer programs are on the market and can be helpful, but be careful of overloading your people.

5. *Using Released Items.* Released items are definitely of great value and can help tremendously. Be careful, though, because some states do not allow the use of released items in any local student assessments. Also, these released items represent the level of understanding required on the summative, end-of-year state test, not the level of understanding required in the first quarter of the year. These items can, however, help local people understand the level of thinking that will be measured on the state assessments.

6. *Having Outside People Do All of the Development.* As discussed earlier, local involvement is critical for the reasons previously stated.

Please don't misunderstand. Some assessment companies do incredible work, but it has been my practice and success to use local people with appropriate resources and help to do this work. Doug Reeves and the Lead and Learn Center are an excellent resource, and his organization was most helpful in my first such project. We used local people to do the actual assessment writing as Reeves's people steered us through the project. Rick Stiggins also does exceptional work in generating local assessments, and I have seen his work as well. Resource D includes a list of people with whom I have worked.

In my experience, what works best is a combination of the above approaches with some outside guidance and help to complete the work. Do make sure that the task force or committee doing the work is aware that these assessments are designed to measure the specific Quarterly Instructional Objectives and nothing more. Do not fall into the trap of extrapolating the content of the assessment items out so far that they somehow reflect the Quarterly Instructional Objectives, but not really. Much work has been devoted to the design of the Power Standards and the Quarterly Instructional Objectives, so make sure you spend the time to develop and use the local assessment system to measure them appropriately. The next section of this chapter will give very specific direction to help you make all of this happen using your own local people.

DOING THE WORK

Again, the original group that did the Power Standards and Quarterly Instructional Objectives or some derivation of it is usually the best group to continue this work. Depending on the size of the district, the group can consist of anything from the entire faculty to a designated curriculum task force. Like most of the other work, this decision will require at least one initial meeting to talk about the project; clarify the goals, roles, and responsibilities; and assign due dates and dates for meetings to check progress. Set aside appropriate staff development funds to cover the cost of the committee work and the work done outside the actual committee meetings. I always gave teachers the option of doing this work in a more comfortable environment, say around a swimming pool or at someone's home. Set a limit to the hours that will be paid for developing the assessments, and work from there. In my experience, this has never been a high-cost item.

In several of the districts I have worked with, assessment development is frequently used as an opportunity for teachers to experiment and try their hand at developing assessments. By allowing teachers who wish to try new things the opportunity to experiment and try things, the development of assessments is accepted as a challenge and learning opportunity. Allowing those who wish to do so the opportunity to develop and pilot assessments removes some of the trepidation from other teachers.

Then, when the first year or semester of the development process is over, the group can take some time during the summer to really work through the process and make major progress. Anyway, relax and enjoy the growing, learning process and the opportunities for growth.

Another common question is, How many items should be on each of the local assessments? While this will vary from grade level to grade level and course to course, be sure the assessment is designed to reflect the content of the Quarterly Instructional Objectives. For example, if the state includes five subskills in math, such as algebraic reasoning, number sense, geometric concepts, integers, and statistics/probability, this should be reflected in the design and numbering of your Quarterly Instructional Objectives. If this phase of the project shows that issue was not appropriately addressed in the development of the Quarterly Instructional Objectives—thank goodness for Plan, Do, Check, Act—we'll fix that right now.

The numbering system used in this process will be incredibly helpful in this stage of the project. Each of the Quarterly Instructional Objectives (3M1.1, etc.) will be assigned a number of specific assessment items, as decided by the grade level or department doing the design of the assessments. You may find out that you have too many Quarterly Instructional Objectives, that you have too few, that one of them is too broad to write items for, and so forth. Again, thank goodness for Plan, Do, Check, Act—that issue, like all of the other issues, will be decided and amended as needed as the system develops and evolves. Your professional learning community is functioning at its best as it learns from its own work.

This reporting/scoring design achieves several purposes. First, because all subskills of the content called math are addressed and measured in each quarter, teachers can visualize what the state is looking for in assessing this area at a particular grade level. How does a kindergarten teacher prepare students for algebraic reasoning? This kind of assessment system helps teachers find that answer, assuming teachers have been given the support and help to understand that issue.

Second, this assessment system designed around subskill (instructional objective) mastery allows teachers to look at student performance based on those subskills, thus making remedial help far more deficit focused. Teachers can quickly see which students did not do well on geometric concepts and make arrangements for tutorial or remedial work based on that specific concept rather than just on a given textbook chapter or failing a test. This approach allows for more flexible grouping and less tracking.

Teachers across a grade level or course can pool students experiencing difficulty with a specific subskill and provide focused tutorials. Students who failed to show proficiency on the second quarter assessment in algebraic reasoning can work on specific remediation strategies with teacher A while those who had trouble with geometric concepts can work on specific remediation strategies with teacher B, and so on. Teacher A can work with those students needing help with vocabulary development while teachers B and C work with those who demonstrated mastery of vocabulary development on enrichment activities around vocabulary. Encourage teachers to work together to find innovative ways to correct deficits; the creativity of the grade-level or course team, coupled with teachers' dedication to kids, will produce effective solutions.

This use of common assessments with subskill scores directly aligned to the Quarterly Instructional Objectives also allows teachers in the same grade level to discuss student performance and learn from each other. If there are four third-grade teachers, and one of those teacher's students scored at 95 percent proficient or better on a certain subskill while the other teachers' students did not fare as well, there is time and reason to talk about why this happened and what other teachers can do to learn from each other—a real demonstration of a professional learning community at work. If all teachers' students did poorly, that tells the group something also. Again, teachers use the Plan, Do, Check, Act cycle to facilitate discussion and teacher learning as well as student learning—we become a true learning community.

But again, the local educational system must provide the time, structure, and support to allow teachers to hold these important conversations and make changes to improve results. Regardless of student results, the system can always learn something from local, common assessments, given that the environment and leadership are present to facilitate these conversations. Leadership cannot and should not expect teachers to do this on their own as best they can. However, given the time and resources, I have found teachers to be very good at using existing time more creatively when they have a reason to do so.

Lisa Carter (2007, p. 49) talks about deckhands on aircraft carriers who "walk the deck" at the end of each day. They walk along the flight deck, shoulder to shoulder, and look for things that could cause problems in landings the next time. While they walk the deck, they process how the day went, what went well and didn't go well, and how they can improve. Leadership in this change process must provide time and structure for teachers to walk the deck and discuss what worked and what didn't. Remember, adults don't learn from doing, adults learn from processing what they have done.

A SAMPLE OF DOING THE WORK

To show you the incredible difference in approach that this system presents, let's walk through an example of developing local assessments. For the sake of continuity, let's again use the third-grade math work done by Morrison, Illinois, as an example. By going to www.partners4results.org/demo, you can see examples of this work at other grade levels and in other subjects. Again, this work was developed by Morrison several years ago as part of this process and continues to go through the continuous improvement loop of Plan, Do, Check, Act to be refined and improved.

THIRD-GRADE MATH POWER STANDARD: 3M

By the end of third grade, the student will be able to

- use counting comparison, estimation, and numeric relationships in whole and fractional numbers;
- demonstrate a knowledge of basic addition, subtraction, and multiplication facts;
- solve one-step problems using multiple-digit addition and subtraction and single-digit multiplication problem–solving strategies;
- use appropriate techniques to determine units of measurement, money, and time; and
- identify geometric shapes.

Third-Grade Math Instructional Objectives: First Quarter

The student will

- 3M1.1—demonstrate basic knowledge of addition facts from 0 to 18;
- 3M1.2—count by 2s, 5s, 10s, and 100s;
- 3M1.3—identify place value of ones and tens;
- 3M1.4—identify a square, rectangle, circle, triangle, trapezoid, polygon, and parallelogram;
- 3M1.5—measure to the nearest inch and centimeter;
- 3M1.6—solve one-step multiple-digit addition problems;
- 3M1.7—count by pennies, nickels, and dimes;
- 3M1.8—tell time to the nearest hour and half hour; and
- 3M1.9—draw and read a bar graph.

Most of the necessary work in coming to understand the state standards and assessment systems was done during the development of the Power Standards and Quarterly Instructional Objectives, so that facet of the process has been addressed. You may or may not feel a need to revisit those pieces during your assessment development stage. As the teachers implement the Quarterly Instructional Objectives, that is, use them as the basis of their instruction during the first year, they get a better understanding of how well designed and practical those Quarterly Instructional Objectives are.

That is why many schools/districts choose to go through an entire year of implementing the Quarterly Instructional Objectives and the Plan, Do, Check, Act cycle to make sure their Quarterly Instructional Objectives are close to what they need before moving into developing their own complete set of common, aligned assessments. These districts allow and encourage groups of teachers to pilot assessments and individual teachers to experiment with the system but do not require the development of the common assessments or their mandatory use in the first year. Either approach can work, and districts can decide as their local circumstances and resources dictate.

With the assumption that these Quarterly Instructional Objectives are well developed enough to warrant the development of the common, aligned assessments, that process becomes relatively easy. As the third-grade teachers look at the Quarterly Instructional Objectives for the first quarter, there are nine of them.

As these same teachers begin to develop the common, aligned assessments, they go through the list of Quarterly Instructional Objectives one by one and develop an appropriate number of assessment items per Quarterly Instructional Objective, say five items each—perhaps too many for third graders but a starting point in this example. For example, 3M1.1—demonstrate basic knowledge of addition facts from 0 to 18—would need to have five assessment items developed for that specific Quarterly Instructional Objective. The number of items and the categories and cut scores are a totally local decision that will change as use of this process continues and is refined.

The decision would then need to be made as to how many items each student must answer correctly to be considered proficient at this Quarterly Instructional Objective. Again, for the sake of discussion, let's say four correct answers would be considered *demonstrating proficiency* on this Quarterly Instructional Objective. Getting all five correct could be classed as *exceeding* the Quarterly Instructional Objective, three correct could be seen as *approaching,* and two or less could be considered *below* on that Quarterly Instructional Objective. These categories and designations are completely up to the local system and should be aligned to the verbiage used by the state in its assessment system when practical. If the state uses three categories, it is better to use those same categories to help children and parents come to a better understanding of the state designations, but that, again, is a completely local decision.

This same process would be followed for Quarterly Instructional Objective 3M1.2—count by 2s, 5s, 10s, and 100s. An appropriate number of assessment items would be developed, cut scores determined, and the same categories applied. The same would then be done with 3M1.3 and so on until the first quarter common, aligned assessment is finished. In this example, that would result in forty-five items, perhaps too many for a third-grade class, perhaps not, but local teachers would make that decision. The assessment can be given in one or two days, fewer items used, or the number of Quarterly Instructional Objectives reduced. Again, this entire process will go through the Plan, Do, Check, Act cycle to allow teachers in the various grade levels and departments to learn from each other and to improve the curriculum and assessments used in this new system.

Now that the first-quarter assessment is designed, it will be used by the building/district in every third-grade classroom in the building/district at the end of the first quarter. By using the numbering system proposed in this process, teachers will not merely be given a count of how many students passed the assessment (the overall score of 70 percent, 65 percent, or whatever the passing score was judged to be); rather, it is now possible for teachers to see not only how many students were proficient or higher on each specific Quarterly Instructional Objective but who those students are. This system also generates a list of all those students who are proficient as well as those who are not proficient on every Quarterly Instructional Objective. The list of those students who are not proficient and therefore need additional work on the particular skill represented by that Quarterly Instructional Objective can then be used by the teacher in a classroom or by the teachers in a grade level in a building to do appropriate regrouping strategies designed around specific skill deficits as demonstrated on the common, aligned assessments. Sample reports are included in Figures 5.1, 5.2, and 5.3.

Teachers now have the ability and the information to specifically identify those students with specific skill deficits and to design instructional interventions targeted at those specific students rather than the entire group. This system readily identifies skill deficits according to very specific instructional objectives, thus making regrouping and reteaching much more possible and productive. Teachers can even combine groups of students who failed to demonstrate proficiency on specific Quarterly Instructional Objectives across grade levels and classrooms. The same can be done for students who are proficient or exceed the expectation. This system identifies specific strengths and weaknesses in specific students and allows for and encourages regrouping strategies that are truly designed for very specific strengths and weaknesses.

Partners4results software can be used to make this process work more efficiently and quickly, especially the reporting of this work. The Student Instructional Objective Analysis (Figure 5.1) and the Instructional Objective Comparison (Figure 5.2), which clearly show which students have and have not mastered which IO, are e-mailed to the teacher within fifteen minutes of the scoring of the assessment. Some buildings/districts choose to develop their own software or reporting programs built on Excel or some other existing program, and this can be made to work. Such local development is very labor intensive, and the development process can be frustrating for the teachers and administrators. Partners4results has software available that is custom designed to this process and can be used rather easily; it is demonstrated at www.partners4results.org/demo. This information is given by classroom, grade level, or course within the building and by grade level or course across the district. Talk about real-time data!

Figure 5.1 Student Instructional Objective Analysis

A white background indicates student mastered the instructional objective

Gray shading indicates student did not master the instructional objective

Cut score: 75 percent

Student Group	Student	Bubblesheet File	Variable in an Equation Possible Points: 2 (%)	Variable in an Expression Possible Points: 10 (%)	Order of Operations Possible Points: 4 (%)	Order of Operations Possible Points: 2 (%)	Display conceptu. Possible Points: 1 (%)	Identify Like Terms Possible Points: 4 (%)	Rewrite and Simplify Possible Points: 5 (%)	Demonstrate the Possible Points: 4 (%)	Identify What Is Possible Points: 5 (%)	Translate Between Possible Points: 5 (%)
1 ☐	Akayla, Kanee	201002121047	100.0	100.0	50.0	50.0	100.0	100.0	100.0	100.0	100.0	100.0
2 ☐	Alexandria, Renee	201002121047	100.0	100.0	40.0	40.0	50.0	50.0	100.0	100.0	0.0	0.0
3 ☐	Alicia, Autumn	201002121047	100.0	90.0	75.0	100.0	100.0	100.0	100.0	100.0	100.0	100.0
4 ☐	Athina, Marie	201002121047	100.0	100.0	80.0	80.0	75.0	75.0	100.0	100.0	100.0	100.0
5 ☐	Bradley, Randall	201002121047	100.0	50.0	50.0	100.0	0.0	100.0	20.0	75.0	60.0	60.0
6 ☐	Brett, Nickolas	201002121047	100.0	60.0	100.0	100.0	0.0	100.0	40.0	100.0	100.0	60.0
7 ☐	Britney, Lynn	201002121047	100.0	70.0	50.0	50.0	0.0	100.0	80.0	75.0	80.0	80.0

(Continued)

Figure 5.1 (Continued)

	Student Group	Student	Bubblesheet File	Variable in an Equation Possible Points: 2 (%)	Variable in an Expression Possible Points: 10 (%)	Order of Operations Possible Points: 2 (%)	Order of Operations Possible Points: 2 (%)	Display conceptu. Possible Points: 1 (%)	Identify Like Terms Possible Points: 4 (%)	Rewrite and Simplify Possible Points: 5 (%)	Demonstrate the Possible Points: 4 (%)	Identify What Is Possible Points: 5 (%)	Translate Between Possible Points: 5 (%)
8	☐	Caleb, Wade	201002121047	100.0	100.0	70.0	70.0	75.0	75.0	100.0	100.0	100.0	100.0
9	☐	Cashmere, Cashmere	201002121047	100.0	60.0	100.0	100.0	100.0	100.0	80.0	100.0	80.0	100.0
10	☐	Cassidy, Leann	201002121047	100.0	60.0	100.0	50.0	0.0	100.0	40.0	50.0	40.0	80.0
11	☐	Christopher, Ali	201002121047	50.0	50.0	75.0	100.0	100.0	100.0	80.0	100.0	100.0	100.0
12	☐	Christopher, Mic	201002121047	100.0	70.0	100.0	50.0	100.0	100.0	40.0	75.0	60.0	80.0
13	☐	Cullen, Alexander	201002121047	100.0	100.0	80.0	80.0	75.0	75.0	100.0	100.0	100.0	100.0
14	☐	Deundra, N	201002121047	50.0	70.0	100.0	100.0	0.0	100.0	60.0	75.0	100.0	60.0
15	☐	Devante, Paul	201002121047	100.0	60.0	100.0	100.0	0.0	100.0	40.0	100.0	60.0	40.0
16	☐	Drake, Alan	201002121047	100.0	50.0	75.0	50.0	0.0	100.0	40.0	75.0	60.0	80.0

	Student Group	Student	Bubblesheet File	Variable in an Equation Possible Points: 2 (%)	Variable in an Expression Possible Points: 10 (%)	Order of Operations Possible Points: 4 (%)	Order of Operations Possible Points: 2 (%)	Display conceptu. Possible Points: 1 (%)	Identify Like Terms Possible Points: 4 (%)	Rewrite and Simplify Possible Points: 5 (%)	Demonstrate the Possible Points: 4 (%)	Identify What Is Possible Points: 5 (%)	Translate Between Possible Points: 5 (%)
17	☐	Dylan, John Henry	201002121047	100.0	60.0	50.0	100.0	0.0	100.0	40.0	50.0	40.0	100.0
18	☐	Dylan, Lee	201002121047	100.0	70.0	50.0	100.0	100.0	100.0	60.0	50.0	80.0	60.0
19	☐	Eryn, Nicole	201002121047	100.0	50.0	75.0	100.0	100.0	75.0	20.0	100.0	60.0	60.0
20	☐	Giorgio, M	201002121047	100.0	100.0	80.0	80.0	75.0	75.0	100.0	100.0	0.0	0.0
21	☐	Isaac, James Elisha	201002121047	100.0	70.0	75.0	100.0	0.0	100.0	40.0	100.0	100.0	60.0
22	☐	Isaiah, Savon	201002121047	100.0	100.0	100.0	100.0	100.0	100.0	100.0	100.0	100.0	100.0
23	☐	Kaitlynn, Elizabeth	201002121047	100.0	80.0	75.0	100.0	0.0	100.0	60.0	100.0	80.0	100.0
24	☐	Kaley, Ann	201002121047	100.0	100.0	70.0	70.0	75.0	75.0	100.0	100.0	100.0	100.0
25	☐	Karah, Janay	201002121047	100.0	70.0	50.0	50.0	0.0	100.0	60.0	100.0	100.0	100.0

Note: All names are pseudonyms.

Figure 5.2 Instructional Objective Comparison

Instructional Objective	Instructional Objective Description	Number of Questions	Number Correct this Section	Percentage Correct this Section	Percentage Correct Teacher	Number of Classes Teacher	Percentage Correct Course Team	Number of Classes Course Term
Algebra I-O1.1	Variable in an equation	2	68	91.9	91.9	2	58.6	7
Algebra I-O1.2	Variable in an expression	10	247	66.8	66.8	2	45.4	7
Algebra I-O1.3	Order of operations	4	111	75.0	75.0	2	56.9	7
Algebra I-O1.4	Order of operations	2	66	89.2	89.2	2	52.8	7
Algebra I-O1.5	Patterns and functions	1	18	48.6	48.6	2	31.0	7
Algebra I-O1.6	Like terms	4	142	95.9	95.9	2	64.1	7
Algebra I-O1.7	Distributive property	5	101	54.6	54.6	2	52.0	7
Algebra I-O1.8	Solving equations	4	118	79.7	79.7	2	67.8	7
Algebra I-O2.3	Rations and proportions	3	75	67.6	67.6	2	57.0	7
Algebra I-O2.5	Percentage of change	2	41	55.4	55.4	2	41.7	7
Algebra I-O2.7	Inequalities	2	51	68.9	68.9	2	67.2	7
Algebra I-O2.10	Function rule	5	122	65.9	65.9	2	62.5	7
Algebra I-O2.11	Function rules, tables, and graphs	5	150	81.1	81.1	2	74.8	7
Algebra I-O2.12	Describing number patterns	7	211	81.5	81.5	2	76.7	7

Figure 5.3 Student Item Analysis

Scored Results

A white background indicates correct answer

Gray shading indicates incorrect answer

	Student Group	Student	Bubblesheet File	Score Date	Possible Points	Points Earned	Percentage	Student Status	Error Count	Missing Answer Count	1 Algebra 1.02.7 Answer: C	2 Algebra 1.02.7 Answer: J	3 Algebra 1.02.12 Answer: C	4 Algebra 1.02.11 Answer: G	5 Algebra 1.02.10 Answer: B	6 Algebra 1.02.11 Answer: G
1	☐	Akayla, Kanee	201002121047	02/12/2010	56	42	75	Y	0	0	C	J	C	G	D	G
2	☐	Alexandria, Renee	201002121047	02/12/2010	56	33	59	Y	0	0	C	H	C	G	B	G
3	☐	Alicia, Autumn	201002121047	02/12/2010	56	54	96	Y	0	0	C	J	C	G	B	G
4	☐	Athina, Marie	201002121047	02/12/2010	56	52	93	Y	0	0	C	J	C	G	B	G
5	☐	Bradley, Randall	201002121047	02/12/2010	56	31	55	Y	0	0	C	G	C	G	B	F
6	☐	Brett, Nickolas	201002121047	02/12/2010	56	42	75	Y	0	0	C	J	C	G	B	G

(Continued)

Figure 5.3 (Continued)

	Student Group	Student	Bubblesheet File	Score Date	Possible Points	Points Earned	Percentage	Student Status	Error Count	Missing Answer Count	1 Algebra 1.02.7 Answer: C	2 Algebra 1.02.7 Answer: J	3 Algebra 1.02.12 Answer: C	4 Algebra 1.02.11 Answer: G	5 Algebra 1.02.10 Answer: B	6 Algebra 1.02.11 Answer: G
7	☐	Britney, Lynn	201002121047	02/12/2010	56	41	73	Y	0	0	C	G	C	G	B	G
8	☐	Caleb, Wade	201002121047	02/12/2010	56	48	86	Y	0	0	C	J	C	G	B	G
9	☐	Cashmere, Cashmere	201002121047	02/12/2010	56	34	61	Y	0	0	B	J	C	G	B	G
10	☐	Cassidy, Leann	201002121047	02/12/2010	56	48	86	Y	0	0	C	J	C	G	B	G
11	☐	Christopher, Ali	201002121047	02/12/2010	56	41	73	Y	0	0	C	J	A	G	B	F
12	☐	Christopher, Mic	201002121047	02/12/2010	56	47	84	Y	0	0	C	G	C	G	B	G
13	☐	Cullen, Alexander	201002121047	02/12/2010	56	43	77	Y	0	0	C	J	C	G	A	H
14	☐	Deundra, N	201002121047	02/12/2010	56	38	68	Y	0	0	C	J	C	G	B	F

	Student Group	Student	Bubblesheet File	Score Date	Possible Points	Points Earned	Percentage	Student Status	Error Count	Missing Answer Count	1 Algebra 1.02.7 Answer: C	2 Algebra 1.02.7 Answer: J	3 Algebra 1.02.12 Answer: C	4 Algebra 1.02.11 Answer: G	5 Algebra 1.02.10 Answer: B	6 Algebra 1.02.11 Answer: G
15	☐	Devante, Paul	201002121047	02/12/2010	56	35	63	Y	0	0	B	H	C	G	A	G
16	☐	Drake, Alan	201002121047	02/12/2010	56	37	66	Y	0	0	B	J	C	G	B	G
17	☐	Dylan, John Henry	201002121047	02/12/2010	56	40	71	Y	0	0	C	G	C	G	A	H
18	☐	Dylan, Lee	201002121047	02/12/2010	56	41	73	Y	0	0	C	J	C	G	B	G
19	☐	Eryn, Nicole	201002121047	02/12/2010	56	45	80	Y	0	1	C	J		G	B	G
20	☐	Giorgio, M	201002121047	02/12/2010	56	43	77	Y	0	0	C	G	C	F	B	G
21	☐	Isaac, James Elisha	201002121047	02/12/2010	56	54	96	Y	0	0	C	J	C	G	B	G
22	☐	Isaiah, Savon						Did Not Take								
23	☐	Kaitlynn, Elizabeth	201002121047	02/12/2010	56	46	82	Y	0	0	C	J	C	G	B	G

Note: All names are pseudonyms.

As with every part of this process, gathering formal feedback is critical. Due to the nature of the quarterly work being done here, you must now gather feedback after every quarter of implementation. How did first-quarter quarterly assessments work? What about second-quarter assessments? One of the feedback forms used in this process is shown in the Feedback Quarterly Assessments: First Quarter box and in Resource C. I have removed some of the spacing for ease of publishing.

FEEDBACK QUARTERLY ASSESSMENTS: FIRST QUARTER

1 is bad; 5 is good.

1. I understand the first-quarter assessments and what I am to do with them.

1	2	3	4	5
Strongly Disagree	Disagree	Neutral	Agree	Strongly Agree

Comments (use back of page if needed):

2. I understand what I am expected to do with the results of the first-quarter assessments.

1	2	3	4	5
Strongly Disagree	Disagree	Neutral	Agree	Strongly Agree

Comments (use back of page if needed):

3. I believe these first-quarter assessments reflect the skills required in the Quarterly Instructional Objectives.

1	2	3	4	5
Strongly Disagree	Disagree	Neutral	Agree	Strongly Agree

Comments (use back of page if needed):

---

4. I believe our students are capable of demonstrating proficiency on these first-quarter assessments.

1	2	3	4	5
Strongly Disagree	Disagree	Neutral	Agree	Strongly Agree

Comments (use back of page if needed):

5. Please suggest any SPECIFIC language changes you would recommend for any of this assessment. Please use the back of the page or additional pages if needed.

Grade Level: _____ Building: _____

Signature (Optional): _____

Again, you are looking for very specific feedback from your teachers: Do they understand what they are to do with the assessments and the results? Do they believe the assessments reflect the skills they taught in the Quarterly Instructional Objectives? Do they believe students are capable of showing proficiency on these assessments? Specific language suggestions are sought, not just "I don't like item number 7." When gathered by the principal or department chair, as they should be, the instructional leader of the building is given very specific feedback that allows him or her to help work through any issues with the staff as part of the solution.

Like the other forms shared in this book, this one should be distributed to the entire staff and collected by the principals or department chairs. Since these assessments are being used on a quarterly basis, the feedback sheets really need to be collected during the year, immediately after the assessments are used. You may choose to not deal with the data they produce at that time of the year, and that is okay. You may choose to save all of the results until the following spring/summer when the task force will meet to revise its work. The important part here is that feedback is put on paper or electronically recorded while the issues are still fresh in the teachers' minds. It is hard to ask someone in May how things went in October. Do these forms every quarter, and save them for the entire task force to deal with.

You may choose to gather, photocopy, and forward these forms to specific grade levels as they are received just to give the various grade levels/departments a chance to look at them while the information is fresh in their minds as well. If these common, aligned assessments are being developed during the year just before they are being used, such immediate feedback can also be used in developing the next quarterly assessments. Here again, the local process will determine what works best.

FURTHER APPLICATIONS OF THE WORK

Not all of the assessments a district develops and uses will be quarterly assessments, so a sample of an assessment of just the first three Quarterly Instructional Objectives from the Third-Grade Math Power Standard: 3M box is presented in the Math Assessment box and in Resource C as a sample of doing this work. You can see how each instructional objective is measured by very specific items—perhaps too many or not enough items, but that can be decided through the Plan, Do, Check, Act cycle. This sample assessment is presented to clearly illustrate the process of locally developed common assessments using local teachers. The items can be developed by teachers, electronically exported from textbook item banks, exported from purchased assessments, or whatever the district chooses to do. But the assessment items measure Quarterly Instructional Objectives, not textbook content. Again, spacing has been removed for ease of publishing.

MATH ASSESSMENT

Name _____

3M1.1. Demonstrate basic knowledge of addition facts from 0 to 18

Add the following equations. Circle the letter of the correct answer.

1. 3 plus 2 =
   A. 7   C. 12
   B. 5   D. 8

2. 8 plus 9 =

    A. 13   C. 21

    B. 17   D. 10

3. 4 plus 6 =

    A. 20   C. 10

    B. 8   D. 2

4. 5 plus 7 =

    A. 9   C. 12

    B. 8   D. 14

5. 8 plus 8 =

    A. 20   C. 16

    B. 15   D. 10

3M1.2. Count by 2s, 5s, 10s, and 100s

Predict the next number in each pattern. Circle the letter of the correct answer.

6. 440, 438, 436, _____, _____

    A. 441, 443   C. 434, 432

    B. 442, 444   D. 437, 438

7. 146, 246, 346, 446, _____

    A. 546   C. 456

    B. 547   D. 448

8. 45, 35, 25, 15, _____

    A. 20   C. 0

    B. 5   D. 50

9. Mary skip counts by 2s to write a number pattern. The first number is 132. The second number is 134. What are the third and fourth numbers?

    A. 122, 124   C. 136, 138

    B. 131, 133   D. 136, 137

10. Rick wrote the following number pattern: 45, 50, 55, 60. What is the eighth number in this pattern?

    A. 85   C. 70

    B. 65   D. 80

(Continued)

(Continued)

3M1.3. Identify place value of ones and tens

Answer the following questions based on number place values. Circle the letter of the correct answer.

11. What is the value of 5 in 45?
    A. 5   C. 500
    B. 50   D. 5,000

12. What is the value of 8 in 80?
    A. 8   C. 800
    B. 8,000   D. 80

13. Which digit in 6,324 has the least value?
    A. 6   C. 2
    B. 4   D. 3

14. Susan made a model using base-ten blocks. She used 8 tens and 7 ones. What number did she model?
    A. 87   C. 807
    B. 78   D. 870

15. Rick used base-ten blocks to model 154. If he takes away 1 ten block what number will his model show?
    A. 164   C. 254
    B. 144   D. 155

Note: Many thanks to Heidi Downing for her work here.

You will note in this example that the actual Quarterly Instructional Objectives are written on the test. I encourage this because the teacher, through regular use of the instructional objectives, has shared these expectations with the kids, so there are no surprises—this is what I told you we would learn, so here is the assessment to measure if you learned those skills.

Further, think of the ability of this system to reduce teachers' workload in the development and use of the weekly or monthly assessments used on a regular basis in the classroom. If teacher A is teaching Quarterly

Instructional Objective Al1.1.1—associative, commutative, and distributive properties—all of the other teachers in that grade level in that building will be teaching that same Quarterly Instructional Objective in a very similar time frame. Why couldn't teacher B and teacher C use the same end-of-unit assessment to measure successful completion of that unit? Why couldn't teachers take turns developing end-of-unit assessments for biology? If the end-of-unit assessment is covering the same Quarterly Instructional Objective(s), why not share assessments? Think of the possibility for reducing teacher workload, not to mention increasing teachers' learning from each other. This whole process holds great potential for helping us become true professional learning communities. The Partners4results software also stores all of these assessments on the district's website for ease of sharing within the district (www.partners4results.org/demo).

PUBLICATION AND STORAGE ISSUES

Another issue to consider in advance of this project is how to publish and store these tests once they are completed. Think about it. There are anywhere from one to thirteen grade levels (although paper-and-pencil tests may not be judged appropriate in the earlier grades), four quarterly assessments (one for each quarter), and assessments in math, English, reading, science, social studies, and all high school courses. The numbers get staggering pretty quickly. The problem is not insurmountable, but it does need to be considered and decided on before the process begins.

The first issue to address is a numbering system. Each assessment should be numbered to distinguish it from all the other assessments; they all look the same when they are stored in a large pile. The numbering system advocated throughout this book is readily applicable to these assessments. First-grade math, first quarter, would be 1-M-1, and so on through the entire list of grade levels and courses. Adopt this numbering system in advance, and be sure all assessments are identified with this common, agreed-to number on every page. Again, the Partners4results software package automatically addresses these issues and is demonstrated at www.partners4results.org/demo.

Who will publish the assessments, that is, which office or secretarial pool? Again, I recommend using a particular office, usually the Project Owner's, or a person who has shown expertise in this area. If everyone agrees to submit the assessments electronically by a deadline, the person in charge can format them and make them look good. The decision may be made to scan some of them if they are in paper format, but make sure to discuss this and decide in advance so everyone knows the expectation.

How will the district store them? I have seen assessments published in paper format and distributed to every teacher just prior to test administration. This is both costly and confusing for the people in charge of publishing and distributing them. I have also seen the assessments stored electronically on a district website where they are password protected. Teachers then go to the website, download the appropriate assessments, print them, and share them among grade levels. This saves lots of paper and hassles, but remember to build adequate photocopying capacity into the building budgets.

Another option is putting all of the district's K–12 assessments on a disk. Teachers then print and photocopy assessments as needed and share them where possible to save paper. Because each solution will raise different issues in a district, I always suggest that appropriate departments get together, especially the technology department, to come up with the best arrangement for the specific building/district within its own resources and limitations.

Whatever decisions are made about how best to publish and store the assessments, just make sure all those who will be involved in implementing the decisions are involved in the design and decision-making phase.

Again, the software program from Partners4results discussed throughout this book and accessible through www.partners4results.org/demo allows for the electronic storage of and access to all assessments, both common (used by all teachers) and individual (developed and used by individual teachers and possibly shared with all teachers) within the website. This allows 24-7 access to and sharing of all curriculum and assessment materials.

Probably the best solution I have seen to the publication/storage issue was in a New Mexico district. The district spent an entire year developing and piloting the Power Standards, Quarterly Instructional Objectives, and quarterly assessments. When the teachers returned to school in August, each grade-level teacher was given a packet with the state standards, Power Standards, Quarterly Instructional Objectives, and common assessments that he or she would be using for the year. The entire packet was there.

That spoke volumes to the teachers. The alignment work was done. The curriculum for the year was ready to go. Forms were included for teachers to provide feedback for the continuous improvement cycle of Plan, Do, Check, Act. The Quarterly Instructional Objectives and assessments very clearly defined what the students were expected to know and be able to do. Teachers knew the expectations and could begin discussing and sharing those with the students and other teachers on the first day. Sharing the assessments with the teachers led to no mistrust; what good would it do them to simply teach their students the test? Teachers want to help students learn, not cheat. If any teacher's students got all the questions right, that would have provoked a discussion about how that happened. In my mind, this district displayed an exceptional use of curriculum and assessment documents.

SCORING AND USING THE DATA

The only part of this assessment phase left is the deployment of the assessments. As discussed earlier, this phase of the project will be conducted in the second or probably third year and may require some easing into as a building/district. To shake out some of the bugs prior to full implementation, the building/district may want to pilot some of the assessments as they are developed to give feedback to the task force charged with creating them. This also allows the classroom teachers to take a look at the assessments being developed and share any concerns.

Another huge commitment is that when these assessments are finalized and fully implemented, they are mandatory for all teachers to use. The assessments are not an option but rather a part of the instructional cycle and the curriculum system that all must abide by and support. Remember, DWYSYWD—do what you said you would do. If this reform agenda is really about systemic change, then leadership is responsible for ensuring the entire system implements the group decision. Like the Quarterly Instructional Objectives and this entire process, these assessments are mandatory, not discretionary.

It may be advisable to leave the grading issue to rest for a while before addressing this potentially controversial issue. Many favor making the assessments, especially at the secondary level, part of the grading system. Because these new assessments serve as the assessments for the courses in question, they could replace the midterm and final exam eventually. However, the school/district may wish to pilot the assessments for a while and work out problems or concerns. That is also fine. Be patient and allow people to come to grips with this new approach.

Right now, while I am working on this manuscript, I have just received a phone call from a principal who is following the system of the Power Standards, Quarterly Instructional Objectives, and quarterly assessments. Several of his teachers are in a panic because they are about to give the common, aligned assessments for the first quarter and realize they have not taught the Quarterly Instructional Objectives for the first quarter; therefore, their students are not ready for the common, aligned assessments. That principal also felt a sense of panic. How could this have happened? Didn't the teachers even read the Quarterly Instructional Objectives? In my own home school district, where we developed these Power Standards and quarterly assessments, I received a similar call from a highly respected teacher. She, too, had not really taught the intended curriculum and was panicked as she realized her students were not prepared for the common, aligned assessments.

(Continued)

(Continued)

In both cases, my advice was to not get too excited. The change process is difficult, and many good teachers are so deeply entrenched in what they have always done that they don't notice the curriculum change. I guess these people believe that what they are teaching *is* the core curriculum. Whatever the reason, it is best to not make a big deal out of this and allow the offending party the dignity of making such a mistake in private. Help the professional staff understand the process and realize that the Power Standards, Quarterly Instructional Objectives, and quarterly assessments are the core of this new system that everyone must use. Trust me; you will laugh about it in the future.

Depending on the format of the quarterly assessments, the scoring of the assessments may be possible by machine or may require hand scoring. If the assessments are going to be scored by hand using a rubric, make sure to do some group scoring to guarantee interrater reliability. That is, develop some group activities within the staff to score some of the common assessments requiring rubrics, and have the staff agree on how to apply the rubric in the same or a similar way. A score of thirty-two, or whatever it may be, should be the same regardless of which teacher issues it.

Many districts that do this group scoring use a common scoring exercise with the entire staff to help staff members better understand the expectations for writing. Simply photocopy a piece of student work, without a student's name, and have the entire faculty score it using the same rubric (preferably the state rubric.) The first time I led this exercise, the group took twenty minutes to score the writing, with a scoring range from seventeen to thirty-one points, that is, somewhere between exemplary and basic. After several more such exercises, the time was cut down to under three minutes, and the range was within two points of agreement—a much better situation. This exercise also helps all teachers better understand the expectations for students.

Remember, in trying to emulate the form and structure of the state assessment, address these design issues in the local assessments and the actual scoring of the local assessments. I also recommend using the same scoring classifications on these common, aligned local assessments that the state uses on its assessments, that is, *meets, exceeds,* and so forth. This also helps students and their parents understand what the scores mean on the state assessment system.

The building/district must also develop a way to record the scores. If the system wants the third-grade teachers to compare scores and walk the deck to discuss the results and implications of the scores, the district must provide a common scoring format that is incorporated into a common reporting form. The same reporting formats will need to be used throughout the district. Again, these reporting formats can be developed in paper or electronic formats. Building/district capabilities are a huge determiner here. When applying this process in a small school or at grade levels, paper-and-pencil reporting formats work well. To apply this work in districts of any real size, it is almost impossible to make it work without some kind of electronic process. The district will need to find technology support to complete this part of the process.

The purpose of the common assessments and scoring exercise is to generate and use formative assessment data to help teachers adjust and improve instruction that helps more students learn and helps students learn more. The turnaround time on scoring these assessments cannot be weeks or months. If data are to be actionable, that is, used by teachers to drive instruction, they must be what Larry Lezotte calls real-time data, not months old. Because local systems vary, the way to turn data around expeditiously is best determined at the local level. The leader's job is to make the data turnaround happen quickly, or teachers will once again feel let down by the system. With the amount of good software out there, there is no reason not to be able to do this, and the Partners4results software explained earlier and demonstrated at www.partners4results.org/demo make this very doable.

It is now time to move on to the complete deployment of this new system and all of the resulting issues. The process will lose most of its linear sequencing from this point forward, and the Plan, Do, Check, Act cycle will replace any linear process—Plan, Do, Check, Act becomes the process. Plan for it, make sure everyone does it, gather feedback on how it went, reflect on that feedback, and redesign as needed.

FINAL THOUGHTS AND USE IN RESPONSE TO INTERVENTION

Through using this curriculum alignment and assessment development process and following the suggestions given here, validity and reliability can be established over time by the faithful application of the work and the Plan, Do, Check, Act process.

Additionally, since this system clearly aligns every item used in the assessments with a Quarterly Instructional Objective and every Quarterly Instructional Objective is clearly aligned to an element of the Power Standards, there is a demonstrated alignment of the assessment items to the state and/or common core standards. Remember, each element of the Power Standards is aligned to a state goal for learning, state standard, common core standard, or whatever the state calls its standards; this clearly demonstrates an alignment of every assessment item to a state standard, thus making these assessments standards-based as well as curriculum-based assessments.

Additionally, these assessments are not scored by individual classroom teachers; rather, they are machine scored or scored through rubrics with interrater reliability established, so they avoid variance in scoring among teachers. These are common assessments, given to all students in a grade level/course and assessing student performance in mastering the state standards that have become the basis for the curriculum and assessment system. Once validity and reliability have been established, through faithful implementation of this process and the constant use of the Plan, Do, Check, Act cycle to ensure items are appropriate, these assessments can now be used in the Response to Intervention process as progress monitors.

These assessments will monitor student progress toward mastering the intended curriculum (state standards), which are now the foundation for the curriculum being taught to every student in the grade level/course. Rather than asking teachers to stop teaching the "real" curriculum and give an outside progress monitor, the new system will use assessments that are based on the actual skills (standards) being taught in the grade level/course at that time. Following this process means these common assessments are now used as assessments for learning and as an integral part of the instruction/assessment/reteaching cycle—a part of the cycle rather than an intrusion into the teaching cycle.

This curriculum/assessment alignment system addresses one of the major concerns of teachers using outside assessment systems—teachers are busy teaching the curriculum they are teaching when someone from outside their classroom or building requires them to stop teaching this perceived "real" curriculum and give an assessment. Since this assessment does not reflect what they have been teaching and the results are not part of the teaching/assessment loop, the teachers, somewhat rightfully, feel their instructional time has been surrendered to give another test, whose use or reason they really don't understand, thus giving assessment its poor reputation in classrooms.

This curriculum/assessment alignment system allows for common, progress-monitoring assessments to be created locally to reflect the actual curriculum that is being taught and to be an integral part of the teaching/ assessment loop, as well it should be. Assessment reports will identify those students who mastered or failed to master Quarterly Instructional Objectives, which are the basis for what was actually taught and should have been learned—now the classroom teacher can use the assessment reports to drive the reteaching loop and to analyze instructional strategies to identify what worked and what did not work. Now the assessment system is truly an integral part of the learning process—assessments *for* learning rather than *of* learning.

PROCESS SUMMARY

The design and creation of the common assessments has begun, and local issues and resources will really drive the sequencing and timing of this work. Make sure you involve your teachers and allow your teachers who are willing and anxious to move forward the opportunity and resources to do so. Take your time and allow the process to unfold as it will in your own system. Through all of the work you have done throughout this process, you really have done and continue to do the work of systemic change—changing the actual system within which the work is done. Be flexible in this final stage, and allow the new system to work while holding that system to the agreed-on timelines and commitments.

Political Issues

During this phase, the political concerns should no longer be as paramount, but teacher concerns about developing and using the common assessments, if pushed too hard, can be a real sticking point, especially in a strong or confrontational union environment. Make sure you are careful and follow guidelines, teacher contracts, and past practice. If extra-duty pay is required to develop common, aligned assessments outside the school day, plan accordingly. Keep everyone informed and comfortable with the project and where it is going. Address any concerns quickly and honestly.

Leadership Issues

The major leadership skills will be working with and understanding teacher concerns as this new common, aligned assessment system is developed. You are really stepping out of the box here and expecting that teachers develop and use the same assessments as their peers in the same grade level or course—this is way out of their experiential base. Help them through this.

There must be a mix of expediency to get the job done and caution to make sure it gets done right. Take your time and listen to concerns. Do not worry if some groups, grade levels, or departments want to jump right on this and get moving—allow that to happen as long as they follow the technical steps, and use them as your study group with the rest of the faculty.

Continuous Improvement Issues

As this third major phase of the project is completed, the continuous improvement processes must also be present in every step. The development of the assessments, like all other phases of the project, requires continued use of Plan, Do, Check, Act—we are in this for the long haul to ensure continuous improvement. This deliberate addressing of the Plan, Do, Check, Act cycle will be closely monitored by your critics and speak volumes to the entire staff about the true reforms being implemented.

Technical Skills

During this phase of the process, the technical skills must again be followed, but their linear nature is really not happening like it did in the earlier stages. Some departments or grade levels will really get excited and get going immediately on developing the common, aligned assessments; others will not. Don't worry about that. Allow those in a hurry to get going, and use their results and learnings as a means to discuss this with the rest of the group. Once the Quarterly Instructional Objectives have been through their first year, , however, it is time to begin the process of developing the common, aligned assessments in earnest. Develop those plans with realistic timelines and reporting formats, and make sure there is a final due date for publication and sharing of the first draft of the common, aligned assessments.

PROCESS CHECKLIST

Make sure you do or consider the following:

❑ Develop the timeline for common assessment development, but do not force every grade level or department to adhere to the same timeline. Some will jump ahead, some will not.

❑ Determine, eventually, the final timeline when all common assessments are to be completed by all grade levels and/or departments included in the initiative.

❑ Determine which courses will be included in the common assessments initiative.

❑ Make sure teachers understand that common, aligned assessments are critical as part of the formative assessments used in the instruction-assessment loop. Provide staff development as needed/indicated.

❑ Ensure teachers understand that the specificity of the Power Standards and Quarterly Instructional Objectives limits the amount of material to be covered.

❑ Facilitate a plan that allows/encourages local teacher involvement in developing common, aligned assessments to the best of the teachers' abilities/preferences.

❏ Before beginning the design phase of the common assessments, the local system must understand the state assessment system and how the state assesses learning—the Project Owner or his or her designee must assume this responsibility.

❏ Make sure to share this state assessment work with the entire task force charged with developing the assessments. This takes time but enhances teachers' abilities to develop aligned assessments.

❏ Every state defines subjects such as reading and math with different sub-skills or component parts that are covered in varying percentages of the state assessment. Know which subskills, and in which proportions, the state assessment is based on, and incorporate this into the development of the district's common, aligned assessments through the Quarterly Instructional Objectives.

❏ Common, aligned assessments should be organized and scored around the numbering system proposed in this book to help teachers and students with the remediation efforts involved in standards-based instruction.

❏ Build in or provide opportunities for reflective time when teachers can walk the deck, that is, process what went well and not so well in the assessment system so they can learn from mistakes and do better next time. This is a great use of staff development days throughout the year.

❏ Discuss and decide on publication and storage issues in advance of finalizing these assessments. Every district has unique issues that need to be addressed before the process is completed.

❏ Make sure plans are made and shared for the collection, collation, and sharing of specific feedback on the common assessments. Keep everyone in the system apprised of progress and issues.

6

Special Concerns and Issues

CHAPTER EXPECTATIONS

In this chapter, I will go through some of the issues revolving around special education, English language learners, and other initial issues that are typically faced in implementing such sweeping curriculum and assessment changes and suggest ways to address some of those issues. While this is not intended to be a complete and comprehensive explanation of those issues, it is intended to give the reader an overview of some of those issues and suggest ways to deal with those issues proactively.

OVERVIEW

The critical issue in this curriculum alignment project is maximizing student learning through a deliberate alignment of the state standards by grade level to what gets taught and when it gets taught. Through this curriculum alignment process, the professional staff has come together as a professional learning community and made agreements about what all students must know and be able to do and when they will learn those things. These commitments to what all students must know and be able to do must apply to all students, not just those who will learn it quickly or easily.

As Larry Lezotte has told us, our mission has changed. We are now about the business of mandatory attendance and mandatory learning for all, a truly challenging and rewarding mission (Lezotte & Cipriano Pepperl, 1999, p. 13). Now we must go to work as a professional learning community to come together and make this learning happen for all of our students, so it is important to discuss some of the issues that are often contentious and particularly problematic for the professional learning community as it strives to make learning for all mandatory.

Applying these academically rigorous standards and assessments that we have created and aligned to the state standards to all of our learners, especially those learners with disabilities or language barriers, is perhaps our greatest challenge and therefore deserves some special discussion. How do we do that? This is a question that plagues many conversations around this issue, but we have to again come together as a professional learning community and do what we need to do and what research and practice have shown us works. There are instructional strategies and methods that do work and that have been shown to work. There are also legal mandates that teachers and districts are required to follow. It is imperative that all professional staff know and understand these mandates as well. These mandates may be accessed through the various state and federal websites and publications dealing with special education issues.

COMMON CURRICULUM AND FORMATIVE ASSESSMENT PRACTICES

Whenever a discussion of standardized curriculum and assessment expectations is held, one of the first questions that comes up is how this will apply to students with disabilities, now sometimes referred to as exceptional education students, and English language learners. This is a really good question and needs to be considered by the Project Owner and the entire system as the program is designed and implemented. This early consideration ensures that these exceptional issues are considered up front and that consensus is reached on how these issues will be addressed.

To adequately frame this discussion, it is important to remember that the major emphasis of this entire initiative is standardizing curriculum and formative assessment expectations across grade levels and courses—to ensure the same standards are taught and assessed across the entire system, including special education and English language learners, and to ensure that third-grade reading and every other course across the district has the same set of curriculum expectations, common formative assessments, and standards in every classroom at approximately the same time of the academic year. This represents a quantum leap for most systems. Those systems doing this work now strive to ensure these expectations are the same across the district, thus creating consensus on learner expectations.

A major advantage for special education teachers is that now all students in the same grade level or course will be exposed to the same set of standards, common formative assessments, and expectations in every classroom in approximately the same time frame. No longer will special education teachers deal with four third-grade students who are experiencing completely different curriculum and assessment systems throughout the year. This will hold true for every class and grade level across the district and will help reduce teacher workload as well as improve student learning. The Quarterly Instructional Objectives will drive what is taught and when it is taught, thus allowing special education teachers to focus their efforts on specific standards-based skills that all students in a grade level or course are expected to learn.

> While we were being visited by a national evaluation team as part of our application for National Blue Ribbon status, one of the examiners asked particularly about how we were including special education students in general education classes. She came back into my office later and told me she had asked several students in several classes how many special education students were in the class and who provided them assistance. Not one of the students told her there were any special education students or teachers in the room. She was curious about whether I had misrepresented what we were doing. I returned with her to those same classrooms and asked the same students the same questions and got the same answers. When I asked those same students who the "extra" teacher helping students was, the students replied, "Oh, that's Mrs. _____. She comes in and helps any kids who are having trouble; she's really cool." None of them knew who the special education students and teacher were—a particularly proud moment in my career.

This standardization of curriculum expectations across classrooms will greatly enhance special education teachers' abilities to work with the regular classroom teachers to develop accommodations and modifications across and among classrooms to better meet the needs of students. This will allow teachers to better collaborate by reducing the variance in content between classrooms. Discussions can now hinge on making accommodations and modifications based on specific, shared curriculum and assessment expectations. Successes and challenges in applying and improving those common approaches can now be shared among teachers as part of the Plan, Do, Check, Act cycle. Additionally, modifications can now be discussed using different Quarterly Instructional Objectives from different grade levels, thus ensuring a standards-based curriculum for all students.

When teachers are teaching the same skills at approximately the same time, those teachers can have conversations about what worked and what didn't work—including and even especially with the students with disabilities and English language learners. The special education teacher now becomes an even more important part of the team delivering instruction and providing accommodations. The special education teacher now works with a team of teachers who are all helping students master the same set of skills.

The observations and work of the special education teacher working with several teachers teaching the same skills becomes especially important to improve those instructional practices. Instructional practices that really worked can now be shared by the special education teacher with the entire team, and important conversations about improving student performance can now be framed in a completely local framework—using local expertise to meet local needs.

Again, this system holds the potential to reduce the teacher workload through creating common, effective solutions to meeting common expectations that are then shared, discussed, and improved through the professional learning communities conversations encouraged by this work. The work of the special education teacher, in concert with the rest of the teacher team, produces better solutions and reduces the individual teacher workload as these successful common strategies are developed and shared among the team.

The opportunities this new system creates for collaboration by special education teachers hold equally true for English language learner teachers. Now that common curriculum and assessment practices are held across grade levels and courses, the same opportunities for cooperation and planning present themselves for English language learner teachers. English language learner teachers can also work with the other teachers to identify and apply strategies that work and that can then be shared with all of the teachers in the professional learning community. Again, the common curriculum and formative assessments hold great promise for improving student learning and reducing teacher workloads.

While working with one of our partners, we were discussing the curriculum expectations for the courses and support systems designed for English language learners and how best to apply the Power Standards and Quarterly Instructional Objectives to these programs. One of the teachers looked at the Power Standards and Quarterly Instructional Objectives for regular foreign language courses and wondered why many of these expectations could not be applied to the English language learner students. If we are trying to help American students better learn the foreign language by also understanding and appreciating the Spanish, French, or whichever culture and communications, why wouldn't we want to do the same thing for English language learner students trying to learn English and the American culture? It proved to be an epiphany as the group was now able to move forward and better verbalize and operationalize its work and goals.

Like much of the work involved in this system, the process of sharing common instructional approaches and interventions and applying them across the grade or course will require work and collaboration over time and will improve as the collaboration becomes part of the new system. The Project Owner and building and departmental leadership must work with teachers to create this new cooperative, collaborative system, but it is worth it and holds great potential for reducing the teacher workload and improving student performance. Remember, this entire system is about change over time through professional involvement and continuous improvement mechanisms. We must create these new systemic approaches and then continuously improve them by processing feedback and input.

LEGAL MANDATES

First and foremost it must be said that the law is quite clear about our obligations and what we are mandated to do to ensure our exceptional learners are successful; however, it is our professional and moral responsibility that really drives this initiative. Just to clarify the legal issues, let's look at some of the legal obligations outlined in current law. A more comprehensive list of pertinent law can be found in other sources, but here are some of the more sweeping requirements to help frame the conversation.

Legally we are required to "maintain high academic achievement standards and clear performance goals for children with disabilities consistent with standards and expectations for all students in the educational system and provide for appropriate and effective strategies and methods to ensure that all children with disabilities have the opportunity to achieve those standards and goals" (Individuals with Disabilities Education Act, section 450-4). Clearly, federal law requires us to maintain high standards for all students to provide effective strategies and methods to ensure children with disabilities have the opportunity to meet those standards. This applies equally to students with disabilities and English language learners. Beyond our moral and professional obligation, we are legally required to make sure this goal is accomplished.

The Individuals with Disabilities Education Act goes on to mandate "having high expectations for such children and ensuring their access to the general education curriculum in the regular classroom . . . and the challenging expectations that have been established for all children . . . providing appropriate special education and related services, and aids and supports in the regular classroom, to such children, whenever appropriate" (Individuals with Disabilities Education Act, section 681-682).

The No Child Left Behind Act mandates academic assessments that provide for "the participation in such assessments of all students and . . . the reasonable adaptations and accommodations for students with disabilities." Therefore, these common, formative assessments that are created by this system must be part of the academic program for all students, including students with disabilities (and English language learner students), and reasonable adaptations and accommodations must be made for students with disabilities.

There are many more citations, I am sure, but the point is made that we are required to set high expectations for all students and then to provide the support and services to help them achieve these goals. That being said, it is important for the reader to realize that there are instructional practices and approaches that have been shown to work and have produced proven results. Again, this is not an exhaustive list but rather a place to begin the discussion, coming to understand that this challenge can be accomplished. Let's move on and discuss how to accomplish this work.

INSTRUCTIONAL STRATEGIES AND METHODS

Power Standards and Quarterly Instructional Objectives provide the high academic standards and clear performance goals required by the federal legislation. So the question becomes, How do we share these instructional strategies and methods that research and fellow educators have shown are successful in meeting the needs of our exceptional learners? Additionally, it is important to share those legal mandates to ensure our professional staff members are informed of their professional and legal obligations.

The answer to this question, like the answer to most instructional issues, is staff development and consensus building around those strategies and methods that have been shown to work. Realize that the staff development being considered here can, but does not have to be, the traditional kind where outside expertise is brought in and all teachers are shown how to implement the strategies and methods. An outside consultant model can be used if the local group feels it is needed, and it can be successful. But let us not delude ourselves that a half day or even an entire day of outside consultant work with the entire staff in a large group setting will move us as far as we need to go to achieve our goal of learning for all.

We must, just like we did with the creation of the Power Standards and Quarterly Instructional Objectives, go about the work of building knowledge of these strategies, methods, and mandates and then go about building consensus on how we will apply these new learnings in our district. As research has shown, staff development in isolation without follow-up coaching and reflection time is not an effective approach to producing change. We need to not only teach our staff the strategies, methods, and mandates but also provide the time and resources for them to apply what they have learned, talk about what works and what gives them problems, and receive feedback from their peers about how better to do what has been identified as critical learning for all. Much like the Plan, Do, Check, Act system applied to the Power Standards and Quarterly Instructional

Objectives, we must build the same kind of continuous improvement loop into the implementation of these strategies, methods, and mandates required to help all children learn.

Additionally, while we may use outside consultants as part of this staff development model, it is imperative to realize that we have lots of local expertise. With the amount of local expertise available within the district, it may very well be possible to use our own local people in providing the initial staff development. Most surely we must use our own people to provide the follow-up coaching and reflection time. How will we deploy our own people to work with our staff to create this local support system that will provide teachers the support and the structure to implement this new, critical initiative? What kinds of structures and supports need to be designed to ensure success? Make sure we build that into the implementation process, complete with feedback and appropriate continuous improvement tools.

Now we go about the work of applying those strategies and practices shown to work by thirty years of research and practice. Meeting the needs of students with disabilities and English language learners, and for that matter all students, is a moral and professional obligation that all educators hold near and dear to their hearts—it is, quite simply, why we became educators: to help all children learn, not just the best and the brightest or the privileged, but all children. For many of our children, we are all that stands between them and the abyss of ignorance. It is our solemn obligation to do all that we can to help them.

Some of the strategies and methods that have been used and researched extensively are listed below. These strategies and methods will most certainly be part of the discussion centering on providing excellent educational services to our exceptional learners. It is imperative that the district assist the entire professional staff in coming to consensus on what these methods mean and how they will be applied in the district. The website www.differentiatedinstruction.com offers several definitions and a place to begin the conversation. For more exhaustive discussions about these issues, you are encouraged to look to other sources.

Differentiated Instruction

Differentiated instruction has long been used as one of the approaches for helping teachers meet the diverse learning needs present in any classroom. Differentiated instruction is a mainstay in meeting the needs of our exceptional learners and directly applies to meeting the needs of students with disabilities and English language learners. The website www.differentiated instruction.com defines differentiated instruction as "an instructional concept that maximizes learning for ALL students regardless of skill level or background. It's based on the fact that in a typical classroom, students vary in their academic abilities, learning styles, personalities, interests, background knowledge and experiences, and levels of motivation for learning." While this definition clarifies the concept of differentiated instruction, it is important to ensure district leadership provide staff development and professional support to internalize and institutionalize its use in the district.

The website www.specialed.about.com/cs/teacherstrategies/a/terminology.htm offers definitions of *accommodations, modifications,* and *strategies,* which are useful in clarifying our resources and ways to help our exceptional learners as well as all of our learners. Go to that website or to any of the numerous textbooks and professional journals for further information or ideas about these and other issues related to serving students with disabilities or English language learners. The point is that there are both legal mandates and resources available to help local educators follow the law and meet their legal, moral, and professional obligations to all learners.

Accommodations

Accommodations "refer to the actual teaching supports and services that the students may require to successfully demonstrate learning. Accommodations should not change expectations to the curriculum grade levels" (www.specialed.about.com/cs/teacherstrategies/a/terminology.htm). Ideas for accommodations can readily be shared among teachers, and the conversation can be facilitated by the special education teacher. Again, leaders need to ensure that accommodations are universally understood and appropriately applied as needed throughout the district. Local special education teachers are, again, a powerful resource. Make sure to provide the time and structure for them to share their expertise.

Modifications

Modifications "refer to changes made to curriculum expectations in order to meet the needs of the student. Modifications are made when the expectations are beyond the student's level of ability. Modifications may be minimal or very complex depending on the student performance. Modifications must be clearly acknowledged in the IEP" (www.specialed.about.com/cs/teacherstrategies/a/terminology.htm).

Strategies

Strategies "refer to skills or techniques used to assist in learning. Strategies are individualized to suit the student learning style and developmental level" (www.specialed.about.com/cs/teacherstrategies/a/terminology.htm).

As districts struggle with implementing Response to Intervention guidelines, this process can be invaluable. As the system of common, formative assessments is developed and refined, the district will identify its own set of both universal screeners and progress monitors. Every student in every grade level and class will be taking the same formative assessments, thus making it possible, over time, to build these assessments to meet the Response to Intervention requirements for both universal screeners and progress monitors. These common, formative assessments will also represent which skills have really been taught as opposed to some outside test that tests skills the teacher may or may not have taught. The skills being taught and assessed will be aligned to the state standards and will represent the level of performance deemed appropriate for that particular time of the academic year.

HOW DO WE BEGIN?

A question that usually arises during this work is how to deal with initial implementation of this new program. The process of developing the Power Standards and Quarterly Instructional Objectives makes it painfully clear for many districts that there has been no common curriculum, assessment practices, or content in the district. The current lack of alignment has created a group of students who are all over the board as far as learning experiences go. If we are going to expose all of our fifth graders to the state fifth-grade standards as reflected in the Power Standards and Quarterly Instructional Objectives, what will we do with those students who were not expected to learn the fourth-grade state standards? And so on, the questions go, from grade level to grade level and from course to course.

Frequently, my first response is, "What do you do with them now?" because the harsh reality is that this issue has gone on for years and has not been dealt with, so it can hardly be used now as an excuse to not move forward with this curriculum alignment process. Regardless of what a district's current or past curriculum expectations were or were not, there will always be variance in student learnings and levels. As discussed above, that is what differentiation, accommodations, and modifications are all about. Thus, it is imperative that teachers receive help with these strategies for dealing with variance within their classrooms and that they be given time and direction to discuss these issues with their peers.

Another frequent response to this issue is the reinforcement of the importance of the Plan, Do, Check, Act cycle so essential to this process. Remember, a critical part of this entire process is formal and regular teacher feedback. The Power Standards and Quarterly Instructional Objectives are then modified to reflect that feedback. The instructional objectives identified in the initial task force work will most certainly need change and refinement based on lots of issues. The instructional objectives first identified and formalized by the task force may be too hard, too easy, too many, too few, too hard to assess, or whatever. That is why this system is built on the Plan, Do, Check, Act cycle; it demands frequent and formal feedback from the teachers, which is then processed by the task force before decisions are made.

When Quarterly Instructional Objectives are judged to need change, the process has a built-in mechanism to ensure that happens. That is what is really meant when people talk about a curriculum's being a living, breathing document. It serves as the basis for all instruction and assessment and is constantly evaluated and revised to reflect the changing student and teacher population as well as the constantly changing and evolving assessment system. We ensure the continuous improvement cycle is used regularly and that changes are made and communicated as deemed appropriate.

PROCESS SUMMARY

This part of the process is really about making sure the group addresses particularly important and potentially contentious issues before they become problems. By openly and honestly discussing these issues as part of the design/implementation process, issues can be clarified and solutions identified. These are critical issues in our mission to ensure learning for all students, so let us make sure the process addresses them early and correctly.

Political Issues

Political issues during this phase will revolve around holding those difficult discussions and seeking solutions with the entire constituency. Special education and English language learner teachers are very valuable resources who can be very helpful if the Project Owner makes sure they are part of the discussion.

Leadership Issues

The major leadership skill will be ensuring the special needs of exceptional learners are considered and discussed as part of the process. How will we meet the needs of these very important learners? Facilitating the conversation and ensuring everyone who needs to be involved is involved and that all members of the learning community are heard and considered is critical.

Continuous Improvement Issues

As in the entire process, continuous improvement is founded on improving the initial work, so creating the best possible initial product that addresses the needs of the exceptional learner and the needs of the transition to the new curriculum and assessment system will be most helpful. Spend the time to do your best work, but assure everyone that the continuous improvement mechanisms will be used to ensure progress.

Technical Skills

During this phase of the process, the technical skills are expressed in making sure the Project Owner is familiar with pertinent law and best practice and in building in continuous improvement. The conversations must be held, and support for and consideration of the learning needs of exceptional learners must be considered.

PROCESS CHECKLIST

Make sure you do or consider the following:

☐ Address the needs of the exceptional learner.

☐ Hold discussions to ensure there is consensus among the professional staff of their obligations to and strategies for dealing with these issues.

☐ Identify staff development needs for implementing this process to meet the needs of exceptional learners.

☐ Design plans to implement the staff development needs.

☐ Identify special needs/problems present in any particular student groups.

☐ Design plans to address these particular group issues/needs.

☐ Consult regularly with special education and English language learner teachers to gauge faculty ability to deal with these programs/issues.

☐ Use the feedback you gather from your teachers to plan yearly staff development programs. The feedback forms will be a rich source of real needs the teachers have expressed for staff development—honor those requests.

☐ Ensure that staff development is provided by competent, respected professionals. These are frequently your own teachers in your own building.

☐ Build buy-in for the program among your faculty by providing them the support they need/request.

☐ Ensure special education and English language learner teachers share the new curriculum and assessment system with the parents of their students and the ways it will be implemented to ensure success by all.

☐ Use faculty and other meeting time to accomplish the new tasks required by the new processes—there is no need to use meeting time to make announcements; do that through e-mails, bulletins, and so forth.

7

Troubleshooting and Follow-Through

CHAPTER EXPECTATIONS

In this chapter, I'll go through the follow-up activities and must-dos for the implementation phase of this, or really any, reform project. The existence of finished and published materials does not guarantee that the project will survive the implementation stage. This chapter gives strategies for overcoming the obstacles to implementation and outlines the critical issues involved in successful implementation, including the importance and use of feedback.

READY, SET, GO! THE FEEDBACK LOOP

And you're off! The documents are completed—that is, the Power Standards, Quarterly Instructional Objectives, and quarterly assessments are developed or in the process of being developed, published, and ready for deployment—so now it is time to make sure the project is successfully implemented and is subject to the continuous improvement loop. The reality is, however, you will probably do the project in steps, so just because you are reading this chapter does not mean the project has even been begun much less finished. That is why this chapter explores obstacles to success, critical deployment issues including feedback, and what to do with that feedback.

As the heart and soul of any continuous improvement process, the Plan, Do, Check, Act cycle must be integrated into the new system. Every single phase of the project, as it is deployed or distributed to staff, must have a feedback loop. Not only should there be a feedback instrument to gather staff feedback; the local educational system must know how to process that feedback, build that feedback into the revision process, and share the compiled feedback and resulting decisions with the entire staff. From the reform initiative's outset, staff involvement and feedback have been hailed as the linchpin of this project, so make sure you follow through on that commitment.

The reform initiative is a massive restructuring of an existing system, a system that has been in place for years, complete with firmly established checks and balances. As members of the system move out of their comfort zones into the new process, concerns or issues have the potential to explode. Therefore, the system must deliberately incorporate a feedback process to address those concerns and new issues. Several of these forms have been explained in previous chapters, and Resource C offers several suggested forms for this use. While these sample forms can provide a good starting place, you will need to tailor the final feedback instruments for your specific project.

Also, there is no such thing as bad feedback unless that feedback is poorly gathered or inaccurately compiled. If the majority of the staff is dissatisfied with the work process or product, the leader and the task force responsible for development and revision need to know—not to get even or teach anyone a lesson but to address legitimate concerns so the entire system can be improved. The staff is involved in a bold, new adventure, and the leaders must listen.

I used to coach swimming and was therefore expected to help judge the diving competition at large events having ten or more teams present. As many as fifteen swim coaches awarded scores for each dive; of course, some of the divers were the coaches' own divers. To resolve this conflict of interest, the highest and lowest scores were automatically eliminated, with the belief that somewhere in between those two scores lay the truth.

What has this got to do with educational reform efforts? As you compile feedback, remember this example—throw out the highest and lowest scores and deal with what is in between. No matter what is done, someone will love it and someone will hate it, but feedback seeks what the group, rather than the individual, feels about the project. That is not to say that any comments should be rejected out of hand, but do not interpret one or two great or terrible scores as the overall reaction. Deal with the concerns openly and honestly, and see what, if anything, the task force can do to fix concerns or expand strengths.

CRITICAL QUESTIONS

Any feedback documents, either those from this book or those developed locally, should reflect and answer the following:

1. *Does the staff understand the new documents and expectations?* That is, do teachers understand the content and meaning of the new documents, Power Standards, Quarterly Instructional Objectives, and quarterly assessments? Have leaders made the expectations for their use crystal clear?

2. *Does the staff believe they are capable of teaching/using the new documents?* Do all staff members believe they have enough expertise and/or training to implement the new practices?

3. *Does the staff believe the students are capable of learning the new expectations?* Does the staff believe the students are capable of meeting/exceeding the new expectations?

4. *Are staff members willing to volunteer to work on the task force to improve the work?* Not everyone will like the new documents, but are the satisfied and dissatisfied staff members willing to help change the documents? Always look for help.

5. *Does the staff believe the documents are appropriate for their grade levels?* Did the task force do the alignment work well? Does the staff believe that these Power Standards and Quarterly Instructional Objectives are really aligned to the state standards? The Plan, Do, Check, Act cycle will be helpful in judging whether these documents truly align to student performance on the summative (state) assessment.

While these questions may seem somewhat obvious, it is important to get a feel for the staff's reaction to the new documents. All teachers must be clear about the expectations and content of these new and very important curriculum and assessment documents. Because leadership cannot merely assume that everyone understands and is able to move forward, regular written feedback can help all staff members feel that they are contributing to this new system. When staff members do not understand a document or its expected use, staff members are not likely to use the documents appropriately. We cannot implement what we do not understand. Give the entire professional staff a chance to tell the task force how to improve its work. In the end, the creation of an open, transparent process will create buy-in and support among the professional staff.

As shown in the sample feedback documents in Resource C and throughout the

> When you dance with the bear, you can't quit when you get tired.
>
> —Russian Proverb

book, the forms present each specific question with a 1 to 5 rating scale and a space below for comments. This allows a secretary or administrative assistant to add up the scores, compute an average score for each item, and tally the count for each numerical response (one 1, three 2s, ten 3s, etc.). These scores are then put on the form along with an exact copy of every comment, spelling errors and all, to each of the questions. These compilations are then returned to the entire staff so everyone knows the group's perception of the new process. If an angry staff member gives poor scores and harsh comments to every single question, that person needs to know the group perception as well—perhaps not every other staff member, or even very many staff members, shares that dissatisfaction, so make sure everyone gets to see the entire data set for the entire building/district. Staff members who are upset need to know whether their feelings reflect mainstream thoughts about the issue.

When asking for feedback about any language contained in the documents, try not to allow general comments, for example, "I hate the Power Standards in third grade." Being upset with a concept (e.g., Power Standards) is very different from being concerned about specific language contained or expectations set in those Power Standards. General comments provide no guidance about what to change, whereas language problems can usually be resolved with better wording. In the feedback process, ask people to offer specific word changes to replace existing language. This allows dissatisfied staff members, and everyone else, to go beyond their anger or discontent and suggest specific alternative wording.

While working with a local district, we designed the end-of-year feedback form for the project. For several very good reasons, the current year of the project was used to create and administer all of the quarterly assessments as the year progressed. First-quarter assessments were developed during the first quarter and administered at the end of first quarter, and so on. Some teachers felt very rushed and unable to do their best work, and several had voiced concerns. The superintendent, who was leaving at the end of the year, was somewhat reticent to include a question about continuing the project for fear the new superintendent would be intimidated by the responses. After some discussion it was decided that we should ask the continuation question because we believed most teachers felt the project was on target. Sure enough, only three teachers of about eighty strongly disagreed with continuing the project—support was overwhelmingly in favor of continuing. Yes, many expressed a need to spend the next year improving and refining the assessments, but the overwhelming sentiment was support for continuing. Such information is invaluable to the new superintendent in dealing with any dissatisfaction expressed by a teacher—the data show support for the project. The data also define our staff development issues for the coming year.

DEALING WITH THE FEEDBACK

As part of this feedback process, the task force responsible for doing the initial work must deal with the feedback and eventually share its decisions with the entire staff. That gives the task force a chance to address the concerns and strengths as a group and devise acceptable improvement strategies. In addition, by ensuring that the building principal gathers and collates the results for his or her building, the process makes sure that the principal knows the specific feelings of building staff on these critical issues. The principal may then share this collated data with the entire staff and work with the school improvement team to develop specific ideas for addressing concerns in the building. Since questions on these feedback forms do not request specific feedback about an individual, there should be no chance for personal attack, nor have I ever seen such personal attacks occur in the feedback process.

> As my dear friend Rachel Pless used to say, Having your say is not having your way!

In my experience, staff members have reacted very positively to these kinds of projects. General feedback at any phase has not been even remotely negative about the process or product. Staff members will sometimes use the feedback process to address old wounds or previous issues, but leaders cannot personalize those matters for which they are not responsible.

> Larry Lezotte says that the best hope for schools is to be found in the fundamental principles of the continuous improvement model.

On the forms I have used, I include a place for a signature, which is optional. My experience has shown that this offers people an option in dealing with issues. Some staff members may legitimately feel previously wronged by the system and do not trust that system to respect opinions or discontent. Allow those folks a chance to give feedback while remaining anonymous. Other staff members may want the leader to know how they feel about these very important issues. Reactions from both the staff who wish to remain anonymous and those who want to be identified are valuable feedback. If anyone in the system has really strong feelings, the task force needs to know that and deal with that appropriately. Dealing with dissatisfaction does not mean revising the entire initiative or stopping the task force's work dead in its tracks; this may mean adjustments, but it is essential to keep the project moving forward. Again, remember Plan, Do, Check, Act as a strategy to try different approaches, see if those approaches work, and move on.

W. Patrick Dolan (1994) observes that to survive, the system must send information up from the level of implementation in an open and constant fashion. To manage successfully, a leader must have people at the point of delivery (in our case, the classroom) who will tell leadership when something is or is not working. It is enormously risky for members of the staff to move "tough" data up the hierarchy, especially in a blaming environment.

Further, there are two questions in a quality environment. Where are the quality indicators (in our case, student performance data)? What is the strategy for getting better? Leadership must get honest, open feedback from members of the organization if the organization is to effectively improve performance.

Probably the most important part of any feedback loop is who makes the final decision. Is the final decision made by vote? By the squeaky wheel? Feedback will offer various solutions and suggestions that must be considered by members of the task force, but the final decision maker is the task force empowered to do the work. This should be stated in the initial conversation about goals, roles, and responsibilities and reiterated throughout the process. When controversial issues arise, as they always do, I have never been a fan of voting. The task force needs to work through the issue until consensus is reached. If consensus cannot be reached, I have sometimes offered the opportunity to kick it up the ladder, which means let someone else decide. That solution has never been accepted.

> Blessed are the flexible, for they shall not be bent out of shape.
>
> —Unknown

Teachers, for the most part, work well together and will go to great lengths to avoid turning issues over to others to decide. Especially in task force work, voting does not prove who is right but who has more friends. Remember, this is a process done by teachers, not a process done to teachers. Additionally, please keep in mind that the Plan, Do, Check, Act cycle will be used to see whether a controversial solution works. As long as the system continues to check to see if things work as designed and correct those things that do not work, opportunities to experiment are given.

The important issue to identify in this review process is what data point, if any, we are trying to address through the intervention strategy (improved student reading scores in vocabulary, attendance, or whatever). Look at that data point to see if it has been positively affected by the change. Solutions either work or don't, so the system must just check to see whether or not the solution worked as planned.

The final point on the feedback loop is building the reporting process right into the feedback documents. When distributing feedback forms, make sure it is clear when the forms are due back, who is to collect them (usually building principals), when and where the committee will process the feedback, and when the feedback will be shared with the entire staff. Honor these communication commitments. Such transparency helps people feel part of that process and more willing to participate.

KEEPING THE PROJECT ALIVE

As everyone in public education knows, lots of programs come and go. This initiative should not be one of them. This is not simply another program but an attempt at systemic reform. This entire process is designed to reform the system and create permanent, positive change. For that to happen, leadership must implement the new system, get continuous feedback, and use the data and feedback to create an even better system.

Always remember this entire process revolves around total quality management and continuous improvement. Create and continuously improve the processes that will be used along with feedback opportunities inherent in a total quality environment to make that systemic change. In following the system proposed in this book and the continuous improvement process, nothing of consequence should happen in any building/district that does not ask for and then process feedback about that action. A staff development day, for example, is a perfect opportunity to get meaningful feedback, and not by using the feedback forms created and sometimes collected by the state. These state forms may be legally required, but they usually serve no internal improvement purpose at all. Also, don't ask if the staff "liked" the inservice—the enjoyment of the inservice is not nearly as important as whether that inservice challenged the staff to think creatively or teach differently to move toward the mission of improved student performance. If a building/district holds an inservice that is not driven by its own data, whose fault is it that staff members see the inservice as irrelevant? A strategic, yearly plan for the improvement of student performance should be in place, with all inservice opportunities integrated into that plan.

> The question is not, "Did I like it?" but rather, "Was it effective?"
>
> —Doug Reeves

If staff members are unhappy with a staff development opportunity, involve them in the selection and choice of future inservice deliveries, knowing full well that working in their rooms is never an option. Again, student performance data should be huge determinants of inservice education, not the fact that someone saw a great speaker at a national conference.

Many of us have been part of or victimized by strategic planning filled with incredible platitudes that produce volumes of work that never gets done. But these documents look good sitting on the shelf in their impressive binders. These massive documents also are impressive to share with the person who asks to see the school improvement plan. One troubled school I worked with had a 66-page school improvement plan that left no stone unturned and created a totally undoable, immeasurable morass for the staff and administration to deal with. Numerous problems and issues were identified yet were not matched with enough time nor resources to resolve them in three years, much less a single year. The document was useless but was mandated by the state as part of the reform initiative.

I also worked in Freeport, Illinois, which has a Plan-on-a-Page. That is right! The entire district plan for the academic year is limited to one page. As the driver of all the school district does, the mission is stated at the top of the page. Four action areas believed to be critical to the achievement of the mission were selected: student performance, equity, human resources, and partnerships. Each area has a set of goals, measures, and action plans. The creation of this document is an inclusive process, and the document is a model of efficiency. Schools are expected to develop their own individual Plans-on-a-Page to emulate and support the district's plan. I have included a copy of the Plan-on-a-Page in Resource A. This document is meaningful, understandable, but most important, doable.

Another issue to zealously guard against is the introduction of another new initiative while this curriculum alignment project is ongoing. This curriculum and assessment project is a process that takes several years. A building/district cannot undertake curriculum alignment this year and then introduce a totally new initiative that will sap the energy and resources from that curriculum alignment project. Data may indicate that literacy strategies are needed to increase reading skills, but that issue must be melded into the overall curriculum alignment project or left for another time. As any decision about new initiatives is made at the local level, be aware of the limited amount of human, financial, and time resources available.

Finally, do not forget the DWYSYWD (do what you said you would do) piece of this entire initiative. Lots of time and energy will be spent to reform the curriculum documents, so what happens next? The principal and other administrative leadership must make sure everyone in every building and classroom is implementing the agreed-on program. A system inspects what it expects, and if teachers never hear the words Power Standards, Quarterly Instructional Objectives, or quarterly assessments except at the opening staff meeting of the school year or at board meetings, teachers quickly learn the reform initiative is not for real. Professional conversations must center on the most important issues that are being dealt with, and leaders are responsible for making sure that happens.

If these Power Standards and Quarterly Instructional Objectives are the core of the instructional planning cycle, how will they be used in the instructional planning process currently in use? Will lesson plans continue to be submitted in the same form and format as they always have been? Will the presence of the Power Standards and Quarterly Instructional Objectives be mandated in some form or format on these required lesson plans? In the classroom? In communication with parents and students? Talk about these decisions with the building staff and come to consensus on what best serves the furtherance of this new system to drive instruction, not what will fill reams of paper and use up more pages of a lesson plan book.

What procedures will be put into place and adhered to by everyone in the system? What kinds of ongoing cycles of review and improvement will be built into the system to use the Plan, Do, Check, Act cycle? What types of feedback opportunities will be provided for the continuous improvement of these documents based on student performance? What works and does not work in the real world of classroom instruction? All of these must be incorporated into the systemic reform.

All of this change requires time and doing things differently. Every building has time set aside for faculty meetings, and it is in these faculty meetings that the staff members can truly become a learning community and discuss as professionals their work and how to improve that work. Make these faculty meetings announcement free—that is, no announcements are allowed—this new system demands that e-mail or faculty bulletins be used to convey everyday announcements that can no longer take up valuable staff learning time. Use the faculty meeting time to discuss important issues and initiatives, and learn together about new and better ways to accomplish building goals and to implement the Power Standards, Quarterly Instructional Objectives, and common assessments. Faculty should not sit for forty minutes to an hour listening to announcements or just listening to really anything. This is valuable time to discuss, explore, decide, reach consensus, and so forth. Guard this time carefully and use it well. Also, department meetings, grade-level meetings, department chair meetings, and so on can be revisioned and used to accomplish and refine this curriculum and assessment work.

If the system is going to inspect what the system expects, then administrators must have a way to do that through classroom visits. In today's market, lots of models of classroom walk-throughs are available, so buildings must choose wisely. What is the purpose of the classroom walk-through? It is certainly not evaluative—all schools and districts have mandated evaluation processes. The purpose of the classroom walk-through is to gather data about what is going on in the building. If we agreed to use the Power Standards and Quarterly Instructional Objectives, how many teachers are, in fact, doing that? Is the entire staff teaching to the state standards? What kinds of instructional strategies are being used? Does one particular instructional strategy dominate?

These and lots of questions need to be answered as efficiently and easily as possible, with data gathering done in a nonjudgmental manner, completely separate from the teacher evaluation model. Classroom walkthroughs should generate data about instructional strategies, teaching the Power Standards and Quarterly Instructional Objectives, and other critical, related instructional issues—information to describe the current reality of instruction within the building. Those data must then be shared with building leadership and the school improvement team so a course of action can be determined to improve those data.

If the data show that the staff is honoring its instructional and curricular commitments, then the school/building knows that the agreed-on curriculum is being taught. If after ensuring the Power Standards and Quarterly Instructional Objectives are being used, no changes take place in student performance, the agreed-on curriculum must, then, be altered and improved. Absent data that the agreed-on curriculum is indeed being used, any effort to change the curriculum can be futile. If the entire staff is not following the same curriculum expectations, how can realistic judgments of that curriculum be made? The critical issue remains—is there a guaranteed curriculum, that is, a curriculum taught by every member of the staff? Until that issue is resolved, real progress in analyzing student performance will be difficult at best.

A model that allows ready access to classroom instructional data needs to be used by the building/district. In short, two- to four-minute visits, the administration can gather data about levels of student engagement, teaching the state standards, instructional strategies, the learning environment, and other key measures. The composite picture that these data create, without the use of teacher names or other identifying information, paints a picture of what is happening in a building. If one hundred visits generate eighty examples of lecture as the primary instructional strategy, that is a data point, not a value judgment but a statement of fact. If eighty of those classrooms have the Power Standards and/or Quarterly Instructional Objectives posted and teachers are teaching to them, that is another data point. Remember, data describe the current reality.

The principal and school improvement team can then look at student performance data, and use those classroom observation data to make decisions. To reform the system, leadership, and in fact all members of that system, must make sure the system is doing what was agreed to. If only half of the teachers are following curriculum alignment expectations, the system cannot be expected to really change. It is leadership's job to monitor and report so all can work together to make reform happen.

FINAL THOUGHTS AND ADVICE

The speed and pace of any implementation plan will vary from building to building and district to district. The critical issue is to not fall victim to the Ready, Aim, Aim, Aim syndrome. The national research is clear—this stuff works, but you gotta do it. People can talk it to death and come up with all kinds of reasons not to do it, but the reality is that systems either do or don't do this curriculum and assessment work based on what those systems and particularly their leadership want to do. There is never enough money! Teachers are always too busy! Other priorities and initiatives are always important!

> Lead, follow, or get out of the way!
>
> —Ted Turner

The harsh reality is, however, that many children are being underserved or poorly served by a curriculum/instruction/ assessment system that is not aligned to anything other than personal preference, textbooks, or tradition. Educators know from mountains of research that these reforms significantly improve student performance, so why aren't these proven reforms being implemented? As Ron Edmonds says, we teachers and administrators became educators because we love kids and care about improving their learning; we now know how to do that, so we can no longer say we would if we knew how. We know how, so let's quit talking and just do it. The references in this and other books identify lots of people who have shown their expertise in making this curriculum and assessment alignment happen all over America in schools just like yours, so use the talent available and get the job done.

The ideas and processes described in this book can be implemented in as few as two staff development days per year with some committee work done during the school year. All districts have at least two staff development days per year, so how are these currently being used? As Larry Lezotte, Doug Reeves, Mike Schmoker, Patrick Dolan, Rick Stiggins, and others have proved, a program will not reform or change an educational system. Real, systemic change does not happen with the introduction of a program (and many, especially experienced teachers, would say "another program"). Real, systemic change occurs when that change reinvents the current system into a new organization that reflects the tenets of total quality management, effective schools, and 90/90/90 schools.

If we choose not to implement proven systemic changes that help more students to learn and help students to learn more, how will we answer when asked what we did during the educational reform movement that swept America in the beginning of the twenty-first century? Will we say we trusted the old way to deliver the new mission of learning for all—even though we knew it didn't work? American public education is facing a crisis, and as leaders, we are responsible for leading public education out of that crisis into what education is capable of achieving: what the educational system did for us, what public education can do for more of America's children if we work to make it happen.

To paraphrase an old adage, the only thing that stands between good and evil is the willingness of a few good people to get involved. For many of America's children, what stands between them and the abyss of ignorance and failure is the willingness of a few good people, you and me, to get involved and reform the system. We became educators to make a difference in children's lives; now is the perfect opportunity to do so. You must ultimately decide whether you will lead or participate in the reform initiative or follow the old, failed way. The crisis in American public education is here, and only you can choose whether you will get involved in the efforts to save public education and the generation of children now in our hands. I hope and pray that you will decide to be part of the solution. We know how to do it; we must now decide to do it. Good luck! May the force be with you.

PROCESS SUMMARY

This part of the process is really about follow-up and follow-through. The groundwork has been laid, and now it is time for the system to continue to move forward based on its own resources and special circumstances. The Plan, Do, Check, Act cycle and the feedback loop will be used extensively and customized to the local district. At this phase of the project, real, systemic change is beginning to happen, so stick with it; you're gaining on it every minute.

Political Issues

Political issues during this phase will revolve around keeping everyone informed about what is going on. There should be no real surprises for anyone, so just keep people informed and treat everyone fairly and as required by state law, past practice, and the teacher contract, if one exists. Remember, it is hard to overcommunicate, so keep everyone informed.

Leadership Issues

The major leadership skills will be developing, using, and sharing feedback instruments to continuously improve the effort and reform the system. Additionally, a major leadership issue during this phase of the project will be to make sure the curriculum commitments made in the development of the Power Standards, Quarterly Instructional Objectives, and common assessments are being honored. After all this work, these commitments must be implemented, and it's everyone's job to make sure they are implemented as designed and subject to the continuous improvement cycle.

Continuous Improvement Issues

As in the entire process, the Plan, Do, Check, Act cycle must be used to monitor and improve the process. Not only do you ensure feedback is gathered; you must make sure the concerns/issues addressed in the feedback are considered, decided on, and acted on by the task force charged with the curriculum area or grade level. These decisions must then be shared with everyone.

Technical Skills

During this phase of the process, the technical skills must again be followed, but their linear nature is, like in the last phase, much less pronounced. The implementation and continuous improvement aspects of this, or any reform initiative, will be a living, changing experience that must be revised and adjusted to fit current realities. Enjoy the challenge and make sure you continuously involve people in that process.

PROCESS CHECKLIST

Make sure you do or consider the following:

☐ Now that the process is being deployed throughout the educational system, the feedback loop and the processing of that feedback are absolutely essential.

☐ The feedback needs to be initially collated at the building level, so the principal has a good feel for the feelings and issues present in his or her building and various departments. This allows the principal to exercise his or her instructional leadership role.

☐ All feedback is considered, but the final decision is made by the task force empowered to do the work. This should have been covered in the initial goals, roles, and responsibilities but should be reiterated just in case.

☐ Remember, feedback from staff should deal with the effectiveness of the reform efforts—are the reforms working as designed? The second issue to be considered is whether the reforms (Power Standards, Quarterly Instructional Objectives, etc.) are affecting student performance as intended. This student performance issue will need to be addressed by looking at test scores, correlations, and so on, which must be part of further study and, perhaps, another book.

(Continued)

(Continued)

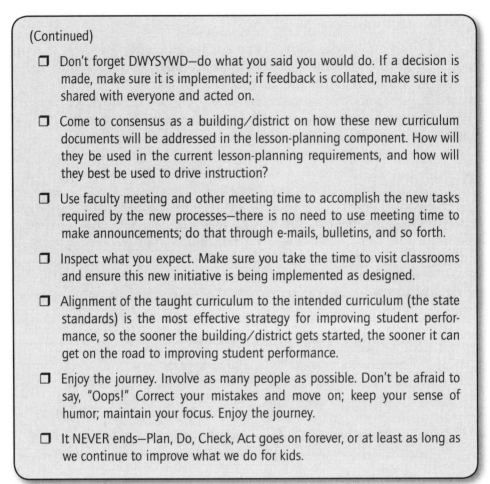

☐ Don't forget DWYSYWD—do what you said you would do. If a decision is made, make sure it is implemented; if feedback is collated, make sure it is shared with everyone and acted on.

☐ Come to consensus as a building/district on how these new curriculum documents will be addressed in the lesson-planning component. How will they be used in the current lesson-planning requirements, and how will they best be used to drive instruction?

☐ Use faculty meeting and other meeting time to accomplish the new tasks required by the new processes—there is no need to use meeting time to make announcements; do that through e-mails, bulletins, and so forth.

☐ Inspect what you expect. Make sure you take the time to visit classrooms and ensure this new initiative is being implemented as designed.

☐ Alignment of the taught curriculum to the intended curriculum (the state standards) is the most effective strategy for improving student performance, so the sooner the building/district gets started, the sooner it can get on the road to improving student performance.

☐ Enjoy the journey. Involve as many people as possible. Don't be afraid to say, "Oops!" Correct your mistakes and move on; keep your sense of humor; maintain your focus. Enjoy the journey.

☐ It NEVER ends—Plan, Do, Check, Act goes on forever, or at least as long as we continue to improve what we do for kids.

Resource A

*Standards-Based Curriculum
Guide Models and Related Documents*

FREEPORT SCHOOL DISTRICT PLAN-ON-A-PAGE

2007–2008

In partnership with students, family and community, we prepare every student for the world of today and tomorrow through excellence in education.

Vision	Goals and Measures	Action Plans
Student Performance — Every student is performing at or above grade level, engaged in his or her learning, and contributing positively to the community.	• By 2010, all students in Grades 3–8 will meet or exceed the ILS as measured by ISAT; by June 2008, 87% of the students will meet or exceed the Reading ILS and 92% will meet or exceed the Math ILS on ISAT. • By June 2014, all students in Grade 11 will meet or exceed the ILS as measured by PSAE; by June 2008, 78% students will meet or exceed the Reading ILS and 63% students will meet or exceed the Math ILS. • For each of the next 4 years, FSD will move at least 10% of students from "meets" to "exceeds" on the State exams. • By June 2010, all grade 8 students will successfully complete Algebra I or a higher level math course. By June 2008, 80% of Grade 7 students will be prepared to successfully complete Algebra I or a higher level math course during the 2008–2009 school year. • By June 2010, close the achievement gap in Grades 3–8, with a greater %age of all groups in the "meets" and "exceeds" categories each year. By June 2008, 81% of African American students in Grades 3–8 will meet or exceed reading ILS and 85% "meet" or "exceed" math ILS. • By June 2014, close the achievement gap for Grades 9–12. By June 2008, 63% of African American high school students will meet or exceed reading and math ILS. • By Sept. 2010, enrollment in high academic courses will mirror the District's ethnic make-up, while low income student group will increase annually 5%age points.	• By Aug. 31, 2007, each school will identify students, below grade level on State exams and/or local assessments, to receive additional support to move students to grade level. • By June 2007, administration will review and improve its process for academic acceleration in student learning, using data/feedback/strategies process, at the District, building, and student levels. The data will be reviewed on a monthly basis, using Literacy First reading assessments (K–6), local reading assessments (K–12), and local math assessments (K–12) to develop student level strategies for improvement in both reading and math. This process will be implemented at the start of the 2007–2008 school year.

Vision	Goals and Measures	Action Plans
↟ **Equity** — Every person is treated fairly, promoting dignity and mutual respect. The diverse talents of all staff and students are fully appreciated and developed.	• By June 2008, African American representation in extra-curricular activities will meet MOU compliance ranges at elementary through high school, and 70% of FJHS and FHS African American students will participate in at least one extra-curricular or "school connecting" activity. • By June 2010, provide a positive learning environment as measured by 100% of staff indicating that they believe schools are safe/secure and atmosphere is conducive for learning. By June 2008, decrease suspensions and conduct referrals by 10%.	• Communicate "it's okay to be smart" message through AVID, Efficacy, student groups, parent meetings, mentoring, etc. • Enroll all grade 6 students who meet/exceed math standards or pass the Orleans math test in Pre-algebra or Algebra I. • Provide staff development in area of cultural diversity. • Counselors and other stakeholders aggressively recruit minorities and low income students for higher level courses. • Aggressively recruit minorities for extra-curricular activities and develop recruitment plans for activities with limited to no diversity. • Continue faithful implementation of Second Step. • Implement PBIS and ICLE Intervention Pyramid as part of the FHS Freshman Plan.
↟ **Partnerships** — Student, family, and community partnerships contribute to the success of every student.	**Student Partnerships** • By June 2008, every student will have a set of personal academic goals that are regularly reviewed and updated at least 4 times/year by students, teachers, and parents. • By June 2008, there will be an increase of 10% of students reporting a safe/caring school environment as measured by survey data.	**Student Partnerships** • Implement a plan at each school to set personal student goals by September 1, 2007. • Establish and maintain a student-focus group at each school to 'listen to' and 'learn from' students. • Implement programs to recognize student success.

(Continued)

(Continued)

Vision	Goals and Measures	Action Plans
	Parent-Family Partnerships • By June, 2010, 90% of District families will have participated in a research-based parent partnership program focused on student success; by June 2008, at least 10% of District families will have participated in a research-based parent partnership program. • By June 2010, at least 90% of parents will express satisfaction with FSD 145 as measured by a District survey.	**Parent-Family Partnerships** • Establish and implement an approach to engage each family in the review and support of their student's goals and plan. • Implement research-based programs to increase parent participation in support of student success. • Implement strategies to gather input from parents regarding their level of satisfaction.
	Community Partnerships • By June 2008, every school will have at least two community partnerships that demonstrate a positive contribution to the physical, social, emotional, and academic growth of students.	**Community Partnerships** • Support each school's efforts to establish effective community partnerships to serve students. • Work with community partners to recruit, train, and sustain an increased number of student mentors.
	Overall • By June 2008, increase public awareness of FSD 145 performance beyond 2007 levels. • By June 2010, at least 90% of a valid community sample will be satisfied with FSD 145.	**Overall** • Establish and implement a comprehensive strategy to enhance school district communications. • Survey a cross-section of community members regarding satisfaction with district programs and services.

Vision	Goals and Measures	Action Plans
Human Resources Our diverse faculty and staff enthusiastically implement best practices and are recognized and valued for our results.	• By August 2010, teaching staff demographics will mirror the Illinois teaching demographics as identified by the State Report Card. • By 2010, the level of African American administrators in the District will have been maintained or increased. • By June 2010, 100% of staff will indicate that they are recognized and valued for district results in student performance, as measured by the annual staff survey. • By June 2010, at least 90% of a valid staff sample will indicate they are satisfied with their work.	• Modify Retention and Recruitment Plan to aggressively increase the number of African American teachers and keep a motivated and highly qualified staff. • Support "Educators for Tomorrow" by providing incentives and encouragement for students, staff, and community members to pursue careers in education. • Evaluate, modify, and aggressively improve the impact of the Staff Recognition Program. • Each school and support service department will analyze its staff survey results and develop conclusions, recommendations, and changes to accelerate improvement. • Provide quality staff development activities for all staff.

Source: Plan-on-a-Page by Freeport School District, 2007, Freeport, IL: Author. Copyright 2007 by the Freeport School District. Reprinted with permission.

Adopted February 21, 2007.

Note: ILS = Illinois standards; ISAT = Illinois Standards Achievement Test; PSAE = Prairie State Academic Evaluation; FSD = Freeport School District; MOU = Memorandum of Understanding between Freeport School District, Freeport Teachers Association, and Freeport African-American Ministers United for Change (to close the gap in learning between blacks and whites); FJHS = Freeport Junior High School; FHS = Freeport High School; AVID = Advancement Via Individual Determination; PBIS = Positive Behavior Intervention and Support; ICLE = International Conference Leadership for Education (Bill Daggett's program).

MUNDELEIN HIGH SCHOOL DISTRICT 120 LONG RANGE PLAN-ON-A-PAGE

2008–2011

The Door to Every Student's Future

Vision	Measures and Goals	Action Plans
Student Achievement and Success To create a culture of rigor and excellence where collaboration leads to the success of all students	• Increase the number of students who meet or exceed standards on PSAE by 10% each year • Increase the number of students who graduate by 5% each year • Increase the number of Latino and African American students enrolled in AP courses by 10% each year • Contact 100% of the parent population annually by MHS staff • Increase and maintain an annual student attendance rate of 95% • Enroll 100% of MHS graduates in post-secondary education, vocational training, or military • Establish a baseline on technology skills and use by students and staff in order to set a growth goal	• Guarantee and support a standard set of academic and social-emotional goals for all students to experience through identified power standards, instructional objectives, and common assessments • Provide rigorous courses in which all students are challenged and engaged • Expose students to literacy strategies in all subject areas • Utilize the data warehouse to track and review individual student performance • Adopt, implement, and assess Illinois State Board of Education technology standards for students and teachers
Facilitation of Learning To provide support for all learners in a high quality educational environment	• Guarantee that 100% of students identified as needing academic, social, and/or emotional support will be served • Implement and maintain the 80/15/5% distribution of students within the Response to Intervention (RtI) model • Increase the number of students who show more than 6 points growth on the EXPLORE, PLAN, and PSAE assessment program • Develop and implement a comprehensive staff development plan that guarantees 100% engagement	• Create an identification process and plan (RtI) for students who struggle academically, socially, and/or emotionally • Create a comprehensive transition plan for incoming 9th graders and their parents • Provide research-based professional development opportunities for all staff • Assess and develop programmatic interventions to address emerging student needs • Enhance articulation with sender districts

Vision	Measures and Goals	Action Plans
	• Develop and administer a freshmen student and parent survey with 100% satisfaction rate with transition plan	• Assess and develop programmatic interventions to address emerging student needs (Tutoring/Summer Bridges; etc.)
Finance and Facilities To obtain funds and maximize utilization of the district's resources for the enhancement of the learning environment	• Increase fund balance by 5% each year • Increase number of days of cash on hand by 30 days • Achieve and maintain Recognition status on the Illinois Financial Profile • Increase the number of core classes (English, Math, Science & Social Studies) with 24 or fewer students • Implement 21st century learning tools in 100% of classrooms and resource areas • Increase by 10% district revenues from alternative sources • Establish baseline on environmentally friendly practices and set a growth goal	• Maintain a balanced budget • Utilize the results of a comprehensive facilities study to determine the potential need for building upgrades and expansion • Implement a staffing model that lowers core class size and addresses the learning needs of all students • Explore and seek alternative revenue sources such as grant and foundation funding • Conduct research to identify state-of-the-art technology tools and provide training for staff use
School and Community Culture To maintain a climate and culture of excellence	• Increase satisfaction of staff, students, parents, and community members incrementally each year • Target student participation to 75% in extra-curricular and athletic activities	• Establish high expectations for trust, respect, responsibility, and communication • Implement events to improve climate by celebrating diversity and unifying the school • Maintain and communicate an effective school safety and crisis management plan • Promote student participation in activities and athletics • Enhance the aesthetics of the building and grounds • Administer an annual climate survey and analyze results to determine the perceptions of staff, students, parents, and community members • Maintain and publicize our student and staff Mustang Pride program to celebrate their contributions

Source: Mundelein High School District 120, Jody Ware, Superintendent.

Note: PSAE = Prairie State Academic Evaluation; AP = Advanced Placement; MHS = Mundelein High School.

Resource B

Sample Power Standards and Quarterly Instructional Objectives

Please note that many of these are first-version Power Standards and Quarterly Instructional Objectives. These will go through the feedback loop and be amended as needed.

From Illinois

Third-Grade Math

By the end of third grade, the student will be able to

- use counting comparison, estimation, and numeric relationships in whole and fractional numbers;
- demonstrate a knowledge of basic addition, subtraction, and multiplication facts;
- solve one-step problems using multiple-digit addition and subtraction and single-digit multiplication problem–solving strategies;
- use appropriate techniques to determine units of measurement, money, and time; and
- identify geometric shapes.

Fifth-Grade Math

When presented with real-life situations, fifth-grade students will collect data and accurately present it on bar, circle, picto-, or line graphs. Students will use estimation, problem-solving strategies, and computational skills to analyze data and predict probabilities. Students will use data to figure range, mean, median, and mode.

Fifth-grade students will use mixed numbers, common fractions, and decimals in addition and subtraction to solve word problems of two or more steps. Students will explain their thinking in writing and number sentences to demonstrate competence in problem solving.

Fifth-grade students will be able to identify two- and three-dimensional geometric shapes and calculate area and perimeter of two-dimensional shapes, using both standard and metric measures. Students will identify symmetry, congruency, and types of angles in geometric figures.

Students will score at least 80 percent on the fifth-grade math benchmark test.

Biology I Power Standards

By the end of Biology I

- Students will use the scientific method to collect, analyze, and draw conclusions from their data. They will present their data and conclusions both graphically and verbally. They will defend results in an oral presentation to their class.
  - By reading about the history of science, students will be able to give examples of how science changes over time.
  - Students will do monthly practice reading for inference and understanding.
  - Students will demonstrate their knowledge of the characteristics of life by being able to examine something given to them and determine its life status.
  - Students will demonstrate their knowledge of ecosystem structure by analyzing an environmental location near school.
  - Students will be able to write a short essay that emphasizes the role of society in science.
  - Students will be able to make an oral presentation that illustrates the role of genetics and evolution in biodiversity.

From New Mexico

Power Standards: Grade 3 Math

3MA Math

By the end of third grade, the student will solve problems using appropriate problem-solving strategies and estimation skills by applying the four basic computation *operations*. The student will demonstrate how to analyze data, formulate questions, and determine *probabilities*; apply appropriate techniques, tools, and formulas to determine measurements; make change using currency; and demonstrate an understanding of geometric concepts and *algebraic applications*, including *relations*, patterns, and *functions*.

State Standards: Grade 3 Math

1A1, 2, 5, 6	Number and number relations (place value, fractions)
1B2, 3, 7; 1C1, 3, 4	Computation
1C3, 4; 4B1	Rounding and estimation
1B1, 4	Operation concepts
4A1, 2, 3, 4; 4B1, 2, 3	Measurement
3A1; 3B1, 2	Geometry and spatial sense
5A1, 2; 5B1; 5C1; 5D2, 3	Data analysis, statistics, and probability
2A1, 2, 3; 2B1	Patterns, functions, algebra
2C1, 2; 5C1, 2	Problem solving and reasoning

Power Standards: High School Math

High School Pre-Algebra (9)

By the end of Pre-Algebra, the student will translate verbal problems to algebraic problems involving whole numbers, solve and graph whole number linear equations, and solve systems of linear equations involving whole numbers.

High School Algebra I (10)

By the end of Algebra I, the student will solve, write, and graph linear equations; translate verbal problems to algebraic problems; solve quadratic and rational equations; and solve systems of linear equations and word problems based on real-world issues. The student will also simplify exponential and square root problems.

High School Geometry (10)

By the end of Geometry, the student will use geometric concepts to classify shapes by characteristics, demonstrate the ability to find dimensional measurements of geometric shapes using acceptable geometric reasoning process, and be proficient in writing geometric proofs.

High School Algebra II (11)

By the end of Algebra II, the student will be able to translate word problems to algebraic problems; solve graphs and write quadratic equations using complex numbers; simplify exponential, radical, and rational expressions; understand the concept of functions; simplify and use matrices; solve and graph conic equations; and understand basic trigonometric ratios using degree and radian measurement.

High School Pre-Calculus

By the end of Pre-Calculus, the student will be able to solve and graph trigonometric functions; factor polynomials higher than degree 2; use the graphing calculator to find minimums, maximums, and zeros of functions; translate graphs; use exponential and logarithmic functions to solve financial problems; and write equations of and solve conic sections.

High School Calculus

By the end of Calculus, the student will be able to evaluate limits, find discontinuity, take derivatives of simple functions, use the chain and power rules, find the area between two curves, and evaluate definite and indefinite integrals.

From Arizona

Power Standards

Reading R-6

By the end of sixth grade, the student will be able to independently read, analyze, and interpret expository, functional, and persuasive texts, including historical and culturally diverse selections at grade level.

Following the reading, students will demonstrate comprehension of elements and aspects of literature by identifying, summarizing, and analyzing selected passages.

Writing/Language W-6

Given a prompt, the student will compose a written essay demonstrating proficiency in the use of the six traits of writing: ideas—content, organization, voice, word choice, sentence fluency, and conventions.

Math M-6

Using the appropriate mathematical operations in real-life situations, sixth-grade students will create or collect, analyze and interpret, display the data using a variety of graphs, and predict future outcomes.

Given problems and real-life situations, sixth-grade students will perform operations of addition, subtraction, multiplication, and division of whole numbers and fractions; calculate the perimeter of given plane geometric figures; and identify given shapes as congruent or similar, with any lines of symmetry.

Students will use algebraic methods to identify and describe patterns and relationships in data, solve problems, and predict outcomes.

From New Mexico

Power Standards

Kindergarten LA Reading

By the end of kindergarten, the student will identify and manipulate letters and sounds in words, associate sounds with letters and use these sounds to read words, identify and produce rhyming words, and identify basic sight words. The student will demonstrate basic comprehension by predicting, drawing conclusions, and sequencing through the use of receptive and expressive language in a variety of ways.

4 LA Reading

By the end of fourth grade, the student will independently read and comprehend selected text at the fourth-grade level. The student will identify and demonstrate use of **reading strategies,** such as rereading the text, paraphrasing, questioning, word identification, and context, to analyze a variety of written information, including critical understanding, **transferring ideas,** predicting, and hypothesizing.

Note: Words in boldface are defined in the district Power Standards document based on New Mexico's definitions.

Algebra I Power Standards

By the end of Algebra I, the student will solve, write, and graph linear equations; translate verbal problems to algebraic problems and solve quadratic and rational equations; and solve systems of linear equations and word problems based on real-world issues. The student will also simplify exponential and square root problems and use data and graphs to estimate and observe patterns.

Sixth-Grade LA Reading

By the end of sixth grade, the student will independently read, comprehend, and analyze selected text at the sixth-grade level. The student will identify and demonstrate use of *reading strategies,* such as interpreting and synthesizing to analyze information by reviewing, restating, and summarizing to determine the importance of, and make connections to, related topics and information.

New Mexico State Standards Used in Developing This Power Standard

1A1	Comprehension
1A1	Vocabulary
1D1, 2, 3, 4, 5	Reading strategies
1A3, 4, 5, 6, 7; 1C1, 2, 3; 1D1; 3B1	Analyze text (literary techniques)
1C1, 2, 3	Evaluate and extending meaning
1B1	Interpret and synthesize

Sixth-Grade LA Writing

By the end of sixth grade, the student will produce a variety of essays demonstrating correct usage of communication *conventions* that present problems and solutions, using simple, *compound, complex*, and *compound-complex* sentences. The student will demonstrate competence in the skill and strategies of the *writing process,* including expressions of individual perspectives.

New Mexico State Standards Used in Developing This Power Standard

| 2B1, 2, 3, 4, 5, 6, 7 | Communication conventions (grammar/language mechanics, sentence structure) |
| 2C1, 2, 3 | Writing strategies (usage, relevance, and supporting sentences) |

Sixth-Grade MA Math

By the end of sixth grade, the student will use appropriate problem-solving strategies and estimation skills to apply the four basic computation *operations* using whole and *rational numbers,* decimals, fractions, and mixed numbers when presented with real-life situations to solve multistep problems. In this problem-solving process, the student will demonstrate how to analyze data, formulate questions, and determine *probabilities.*

By the end of the sixth grade, the student will apply appropriate techniques, tools, and formulas to determine measurements.

By the end of the sixth grade, the student will demonstrate an understanding of geometric concepts and algebra *applications,* including *relations,* patterns, and *functions.*

New Mexico State Standards Used in Developing This Power Standard

1A1, 2, 3, 4, 5; 1B3; 2D2, 4, 5	Number and number relations (percents, ratios)
1B5; 1C7	Operation concepts
1B1, 2, 4, 5, 6; 1C7	Computation
1C1, 2, 3, 5	Estimation
2A1, 2, 3, 4, 5; 2B1, 2, 3, 4, 5; 2C1, 2; 2D1, 2, 3, 4, 5	Patterns, functions, algebra
3A1, 2, 3, 4, 5, 6, 7; 3B1; 3C1; 3D1	Geometry and spatial sense
4A1, 2, 3, 4; 4B1, 2, 3, 4	Measurement
5A1, 2, 3, 4, 5, 6 7, 8, 9, 10, 11; 5B1, 2, 3, 4, 5, 6, 7, 8; 5C1, 2, 3, 4; 5D1, 2, 3, 4, 5, 6, 7	Data analysis, statistics, and probability
1B4; 1C7; 5A5	Problem solving and reasoning

Resource C

Suggested Forms for Developing Power Standards,
Instructional Objectives, and Feedback

STANDARDS TO POWER
STANDARDS DISCUSSION GUIDE

1. Look at the list of standards, benchmarks, and content standards.

2. Look at the state assessments and No Child Left Behind Act—for what are we as educators being held accountable?

3. Determine the skill (noun) students are expected to master and what they are to do with that skill (verb).

4. Determine the most important, most critical skills to demonstrate mastery of the state standard.

5. Can these be combined with other skills to create a more singular Power Standard element?

6. How many skills are so critical that they need to be included in the Power Standard elements?

7. What is the maximum number of Power Standard elements that will give our colleagues the instructional focus to ensure student mastery?

8. Write the Power Standard elements, and relate those elements to specific state goals—remember, a learnable amount.

FOLLOW-UP PROCESS GUIDELINES: POWER STANDARDS

This group may not answer all of these questions today. We should begin the discussion today and develop a process with dates to ensure this work gets decided and completed. With time and commitment, this will become part of a yearly cycle that will ensure the curriculum is always under review and continually improved. The first year or so will be a bit more difficult as timelines are set and processes for review and revision are established. Please be patient and help by being part of the solution. Share your ideas and help us continually improve. The Plan cycle was completed by the work of this group; now we must make sure we follow up with the Do, Check, and Act cycles.

Do Cycle

- When will the Power Standards be due?
- To whom?
- In what format? Electronic? On a form?
- What will they look like? Decide now or later.
- Will the task force/faculty see them prior to final publication? When? Meeting called by whom?
- When will they be published and distributed to staff? By whom? Any follow-up activity by the task force as part of the distribution?

Check Cycle

- When will we gather initial feedback on the Power Standards?
- Who will gather and collate?
- Will we allow midcourse corrections or stick with the initial product for the first year?
- When will we gather end-of-year feedback? From whom? How?

Act Cycle

- When will we meet to review the feedback and make improvements and corrections?
- When and how will we release this second version (and subsequent versions)?

FOLLOW-UP PROCESS GUIDELINES: INSTRUCTIONAL OBJECTIVES

This group may not answer all of these questions today. We should begin the discussion today and develop a process with dates to ensure this work gets decided on and completed. With time and commitment, this will become part of a yearly cycle that will allow the curriculum to always be under review and continually improved. The first year or so will be a bit more difficult as timelines are set and processes for review and revision are established. Please be patient and help by being part of the solution. Share your ideas and help us continually improve.

The Plan cycle was completed by the work of this group; now we must make sure we follow up with the Do, Check, and Act cycles.

Do Cycle

- When will the Quarterly Instructional Objectives be due?
- To whom?
- In what format? Electronic? On a form?
- What will they look like? Numbering system? 8LA1, 7M2?
- Will the task force see them prior to final publication? When? Meeting called by whom?
- When will they be published and distributed to staff? By whom? Any follow-up activity by the task force as part of the distribution?

Check Cycle

- When will we gather initial feedback about the Power Standards and Quarterly Instructional Objectives?
- Who will gather and collate?
- Will we allow midcourse corrections or stick with the initial product for the first year?
- When will we gather end-of-year feedback? By whom? How?

Act Cycle

- When will we meet to review the feedback and make improvements and corrections?
- When and how will we release this second version (and subsequent versions)?

INITIAL DISTRIBUTION FEEDBACK

1 is bad; 5 is good.

1. I understand the Power Standards and Quarterly Instructional Objectives.

1	2	3	4	5
Strongly Disagree	Disagree	Neutral	Agree	Strongly Agree

Comments (use back of page if needed):

2. I understand what I am expected to do with the new Power Standards and Quarterly Instructional Objectives.

1	2	3	4	5
Strongly Disagree	Disagree	Neutral	Agree	Strongly Agree

Comments (use back of page if needed):

3. I believe I am capable of teaching the Power Standards and Quarterly Instructional Objectives.

1	2	3	4	5
Strongly Disagree	Disagree	Neutral	Agree	Strongly Agree

Comments (use back of page if needed):

4. I believe our students are capable of learning these Power Standards and Quarterly Instructional objectives in the grade level to which these standards are assigned.

1	2	3	4	5
Strongly Disagree	Disagree	Neutral	Agree	Strongly Agree

Comments (use back of page if needed):

5. I would be willing to volunteer to work with the Power Standards task force to continue and improve this work.

1	2	3	4	5
Strongly Disagree	Disagree	Neutral	Agree	Strongly Agree

Comments (use back of page if needed):

Grade Level: _____ Building: _____

Signature (Optional): _____

FEEDBACK QUARTERLY ASSESSMENTS: FIRST QUARTER

1 is bad; 5 is good.

1. I understand the first-quarter assessments and what I am to do with them.

1	2	3	4	5
Strongly Disagree	Disagree	Neutral	Agree	Strongly Agree

Comments (use back of page if needed):

2. I understand what I am expected to do with the results of the first-quarter assessments.

1	2	3	4	5
Strongly Disagree	Disagree	Neutral	Agree	Strongly Agree

Comments (use back of page if needed):

3. I believe these first-quarter assessments reflect the skills required in the Quarterly Instructional Objectives.

1	2	3	4	5
Strongly Disagree	Disagree	Neutral	Agree	Strongly Agree

Comments (use back of page if needed):

4. I believe our students are capable of demonstrating proficiency on these first-quarter assessments.

1	2	3	4	5
Strongly Disagree	Disagree	Neutral	Agree	Strongly Agree

Comments (use back of page if needed):

5. Please suggest any SPECIFIC language changes you would recommend for any of this assessment. Please use the back of the page or additional pages if needed.

Grade Level: _____ Building: _____

Signature (Optional): _____

END-OF-YEAR FEEDBACK

As you are well aware, we developed and implemented the Power Standards and Quarterly Instructional Objectives this year. As part of our total quality cycle, it is important to get feedback about how well these are working. We want to know your reaction to the Power Standards and Quarterly Instructional Objectives. To that end, please take a few moments to answer the questions below as they relate to the Power Standards and Quarterly Instructional Objectives you use. We will use your input to look at them and decide which, if any, changes are needed. Please return this form to your building principal. Feel free to work with other members at your grade level/in your department to discuss ideas.

1 is bad; 5 is good.

1. The Power Standards and Quarterly Instructional Objectives for my grade level are realistic and reflect what students should know and be able to do.

1	2	3	4	5
Strongly Disagree	Disagree	Neutral	Agree	Strongly Agree

   Comments (use back of page if needed):

2. The Power Standards and Quarterly Instructional Objectives relate to the skills and expectations in the curriculum guide.

1	2	3	4	5
Strongly Disagree	Disagree	Neutral	Agree	Strongly Agree

   Comments (use back of page if needed):

3. My students are making acceptable progress toward these Power Standards.

1	2	3	4	5
Strongly Disagree	Disagree	Neutral	Agree	Strongly Agree

   Comments (use back of page if needed):

4. I understand the Quarterly Instructional Objectives and am able to tie my instruction to them.

1	2	3	4	5
Strongly Disagree	Disagree	Neutral	Agree	Strongly Agree

Comments (use back of page if needed):

5. My instruction is guided by the Power Standards and Quarterly Instructional Objectives.

1	2	3	4	5
Strongly Disagree	Disagree	Neutral	Agree	Strongly Agree

Comments (use back of page if needed):

6. I understand the Power Standards and Quarterly Instructional Objectives and need no further clarification of them.

1	2	3	4	5
Strongly Disagree	Disagree	Neutral	Agree	Strongly Agree

Comments (use back of page if needed):

Please list below (feel free to use the back of the page if needed) any SPECIFIC changes in the wording of the Power Standards or Quarterly Instructional Objectives that you would suggest.

Grade Level:_____ Building:_____

Signature (Optional): _____

MATH ASSESSMENT

Name _____

3M1.1. Demonstrate basic knowledge of addition facts from 0 to 18

Add the following equations. Circle the letter of the correct answer.

1. 3 plus 2 =
   A. 7   C. 12
   B. 5   D. 8

2. 8 plus 9 =
   A. 13   C. 21
   B. 17   D. 10

3. 4 plus 6 =
   A. 20   C. 10
   B. 8   D. 2

4. 5 plus 7 =
   A. 9   C. 12
   B. 8   D. 14

5. 8 plus 8 =
   A. 20   C. 16
   B. 15   D. 10

3M1.2. Count by 2s, 5s, 10s, and 100s

Predict the next number in each pattern. Circle the letter of the correct answer.

6. 440, 438, 436, _____, _____
   A. 441, 443   C. 434, 432
   B. 442, 444   D. 437, 438

7. 146, 246, 346, 446, _____
   A. 546   C. 456
   B. 547   D. 448

8. 45, 35, 25, 15, _____
   A. 20   C. 0
   B. 5   D. 50

9. Mary skip counts by 2s to write a number pattern. The first number is 132. The second number is 134. What are the third and fourth numbers?

   A. 122, 124   C. 136, 138

   B. 131, 133   D. 136, 137

10. Rick wrote the following number pattern: 45, 50, 55, 60. What is the eighth number in this pattern?

    A. 85   C. 70

    B. 65   D. 80

3M1.3. Identify place value of ones and tens

Answer the following questions based on number place values. Circle the letter of the correct answer.

11. What is the value of 5 in 45?

    A. 5   C. 500

    B. 50   D. 5,000

12. What is the value of 8 in 80?

    A. 8   C. 800

    B. 8,000   D. 80

13. Which digit in 6,324 has the least value?

    A. 6   C. 2

    B. 4   D. 3

14. Susan made a model using base-ten blocks. She used 8 tens and 7 ones. What number did she model?

    A. 87   C. 807

    B. 78   D. 870

15. Rick used base-ten blocks to model 154. If he takes away 1 ten block what number will his model show?

    A. 164   C. 254

    B. 144   D. 155

Note: Many thanks to Heidi Downing for her work here.

Resource D

Recommended Agency References

The Leadership and Learning Center

Contact: Doug Reeves

Address: 317 Inverness Way S., Suite 150, Englewood, CO 80112

Phone: (866) 399-6019

Website: www.leadandlearn.com

Products Offered: The originator of the entire Power Standards movement and the 90/90/90 schools research that shows all children can and must learn

Effective Schools, Ltd.

Address: P.O. Box 1337, Okemos, MI 48805

Phone: (800) 827-8041

Website: www.effectiveschools.com

Products Offered: The original research-proven application of strategies that work to improve learning for all

Assessment Training Institute

Contact: Rick Stiggins

Address: 317 S.W. Alder, Suite 1200, Portland, OR 97204

Phone: (800) 348-4474

Website: www.assessmentinst.com

Products Offered: Help with assessments, both formative and summative, and work with teachers in understanding and applying the instructional/ assessment cycle

Feaver, Inc.

Contact: Lynn Feaver

Address: 3003 W. Forest Rd., Freeport, IL 61032

Phone: (815) 235-9530

E-mail: lynnfeaver@insightbb.com

Services Offered: Help organizations and communities with planning, alignment, measurement systems, performance improvement, and leadership development, all aimed at achieving better results.

Mastery Math

Contact: John Booth

Address: 13518 Medlock Drive, Litchfield Park, AZ 85430

Phone: (623) 979-5892

Fax: (623) 979-6177

E-mail: jabooth@cox.net

Services Offered: High school math alignment and curriculum and assessment work as well as a research-proven product to improve student performance in algebra

Partners4results

Contact: Jim Serpe

Address: 1231 S. Rochester St., Suite 140, Mukwonago, WI 53149

Phone: (414) 704-4227

E-mail: jim@partners4results.org

Website: www.partners4results.org

Services Offered: Software and Internet hosting to complete the entire Power Standards to Quarterly Instructional Objectives at no charge, software to develop and analyze common assessments aligned to the Quarterly Instructional Objectives and Power Standards available for purchase

Resource E

Sample Results

The following charts represent results achieved by schools using the methods advocated in this book. These are real results achieved by real schools with real students and real teachers in the real world.

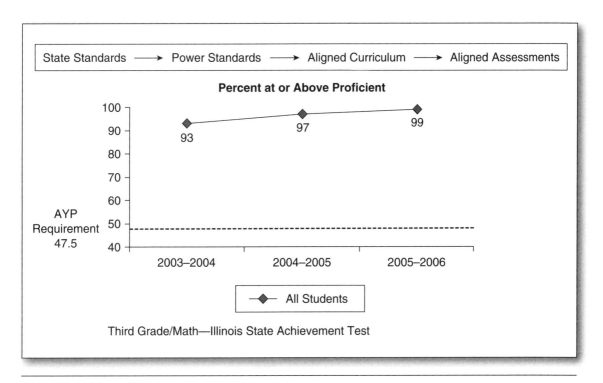

State Standards ⟶ Power Standards ⟶ Aligned Curriculum ⟶ Aligned Assessments

Percent at or Above Proficient

Third Grade/Math—Illinois State Achievement Test

Note: AYP = Adequate Yearly Progress.

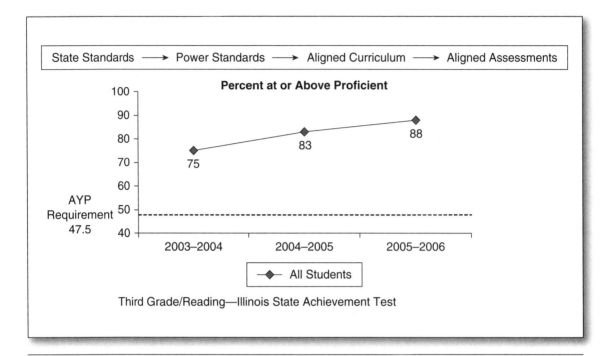

Note: AYP = Adequate Yearly Progress.

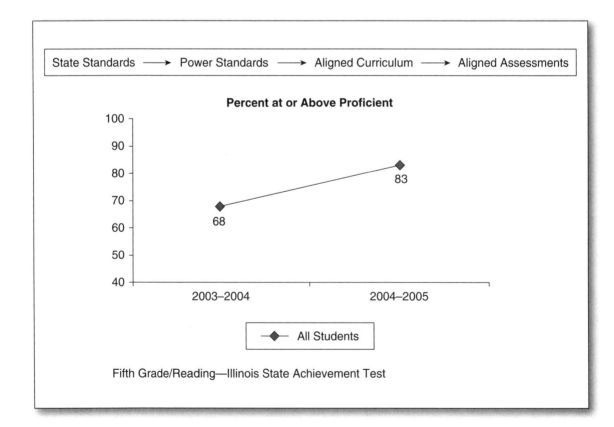

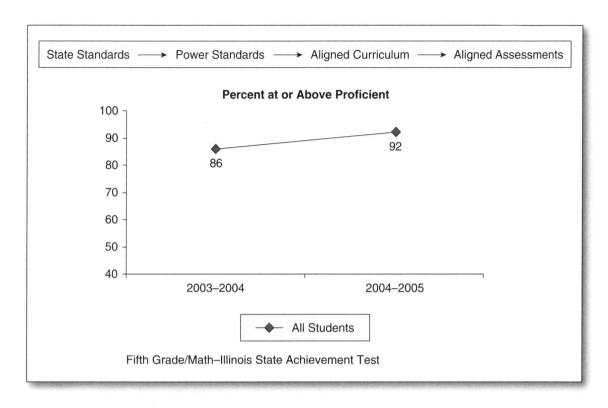

State Standards ⟶ Power Standards ⟶ Aligned Curriculum ⟶ Aligned Assessments

Percent at or Above Proficient

Fifth Grade/Math–Illinois State Achievement Test

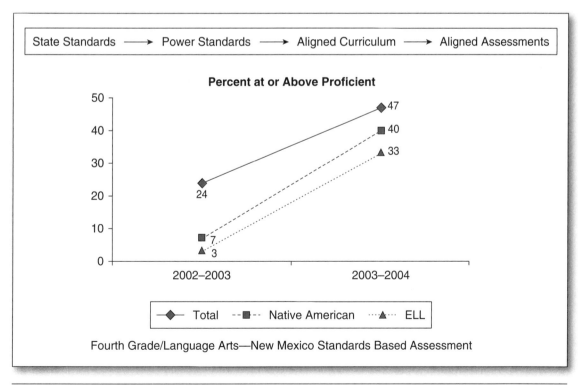

State Standards ⟶ Power Standards ⟶ Aligned Curriculum ⟶ Aligned Assessments

Percent at or Above Proficient

Fourth Grade/Language Arts—New Mexico Standards Based Assessment

Note: ELL = English language learner.

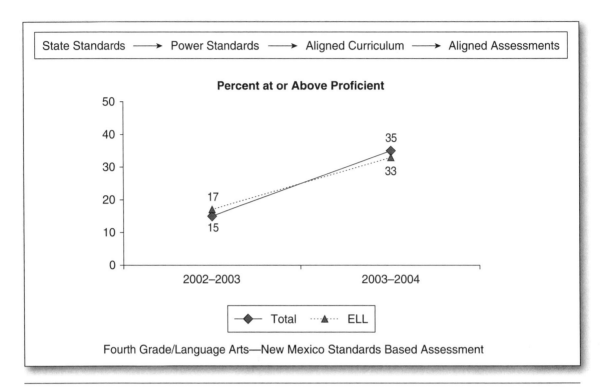

Note: ELL = English language learner.

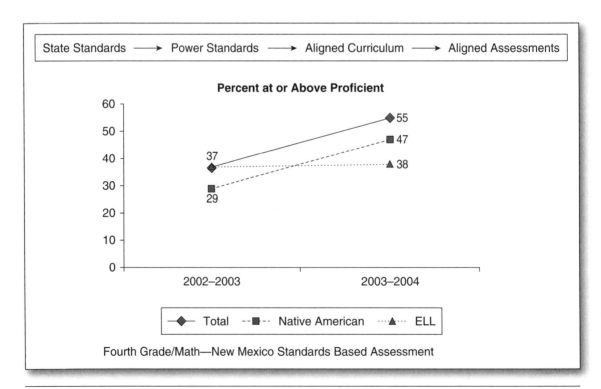

Note: ELL = English language learner.

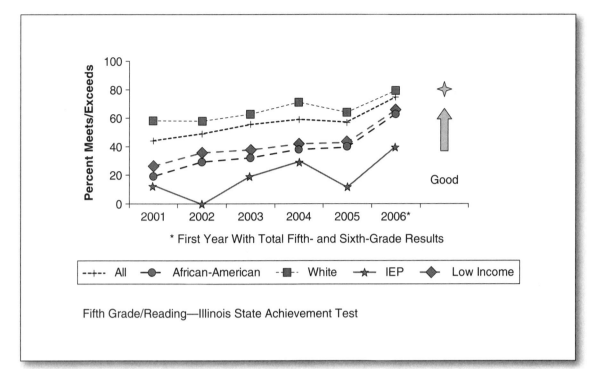

Fifth Grade/Reading—Illinois State Achievement Test

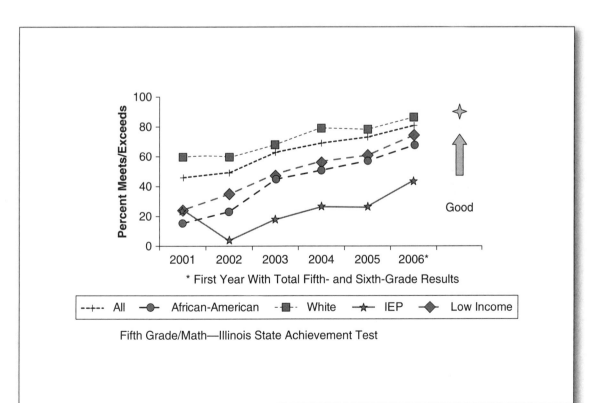

Fifth Grade/Math—Illinois State Achievement Test

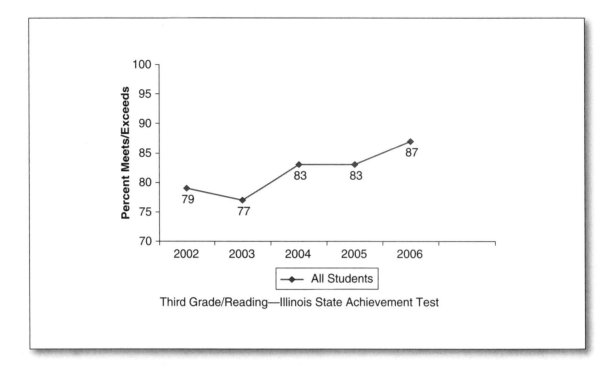

Third Grade/Reading—Illinois State Achievement Test

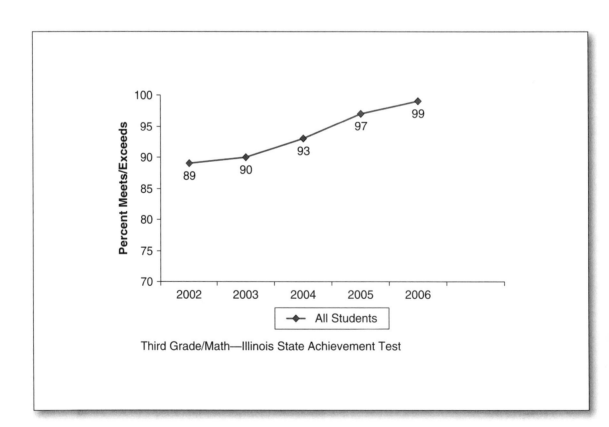

Third Grade/Math—Illinois State Achievement Test

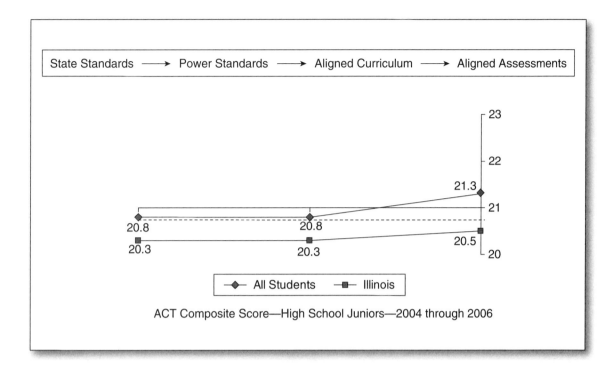

ACT Composite Score—High School Juniors—2004 through 2006

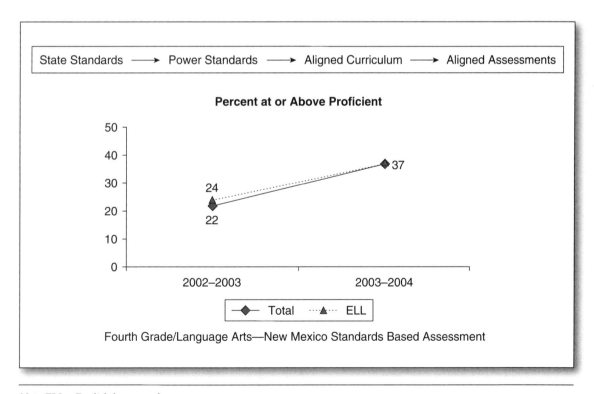

Fourth Grade/Language Arts—New Mexico Standards Based Assessment

Note: ELL = English language learner.

References and Suggested Readings

Ainsworth, L. (2003a). *Power standards: Identifying the standards that matter the most.* Englewood, CO: Advanced Learning Press.

Ainsworth, L. (2003b). *"Unwrapping" the standards.* Englewood, CO: Advanced Learning Press.

Allington, R. L., & Cunningham, P. M. (1996). *Schools that work: Where all children read and write.* New York, NY: HarperCollins.

Barth, R. S. (1990). *Improving schools from within.* San Francisco, CA: Jossey-Bass.

Bliss, J. R., Firestone, W. A., & Richards, C. E. (Eds.). (1991). *Rethinking effective schools: Research and practice.* Englewood Cliffs, NJ: Prentice Hall.

Block, P. (1987). *The empowered manager: Positive political skills at work.* San Francisco, CA: Jossey-Bass.

Bullard, P., & Taylor, B. O. (1993). *Keepers of the dream: The triumph of effective schools.* Chicago, IL: Excelsior.

Carter, L. (2007). *Total instructional alignment: From standards to student success.* Bloomington, IN: Solution Tree.

Clinton, B. (2005). *My life.* New York, NY: Vintage.

Covey, S. R. (1989). *The 7 habits of highly effective people.* Touchstone, NY: Simon & Schuster.

Covey, S. R. (1990). *Principle-centered leadership.* New York, NY: Summit Books.

Darling-Hammond, L. (1997). *The right to learn.* San Francisco, CA: Jossey-Bass.

Deming, W. E. (1989). *Out of the crisis.* Cambridge: Massachusetts Institute of Technology, Center for Advanced Engineering Study.

Deming, W. E. (1993). *The new economics.* Cambridge: Massachusetts Institute of Technology, Center for Advanced Engineering Study.

Dolan, W. P. (1994). *Restructuring our schools: A primer on systemic change.* Kansas City, MO: Systems & Organization.

DuFour, R., & DuFour, B. (2004, September 29). *Professional learning communities.* Workshop presented in Denver, CO.

DuFour, R., & Eaker, R. (1998). *Professional learning communities at work: Best practices for enhancing student achievement.* Bloomington, IA: National Education Service.

Kouzes, J. M., & Posner, B. Z. (1993). *Credibility: How leaders gain and lose it, why people demand it.* San Francisco, CA: Jossey-Bass.

Levine, D. U., & Lezotte, L. W. (1990). *Unusually effective schools: A review and analysis of research and practice.* Madison, WI: National Center for Effective Schools Research & Development.

Lezotte, L. W. (1992). *Creating the total quality effective school.* Okemos, MI: Effective Schools Products.

Lezotte, L. W. (1997). *Learning for all.* Okemos, MI: Effective Schools Products.

Lezotte, L. W., & Cipriano Pepperl, J.-A. (1999). *What the effective schools research says: Safe and orderly environment.* Okemos, MI: Effective Schools Products.

Lezotte, L. W., & Jacoby, B. C. (1992). *Sustainable school reform: The district context for school improvement.* Okemos, MI: Effective Schools Products.

Lezotte, L. W., & McKee, K. (2006). *Stepping up: Leading the charge to improve our schools.* Okemos, MI: Effective Schools Products.

Lezotte, L. W., et al. (1986–present). [Various topics]. *Effective schools research abstracts.* Okemos, MI: Effective Schools Products.

Marzano, R. J. (2007). *The art and science of teaching.* Alexandria, VA: Association for Supervision and Curriculum Development.

Mathews, J. (1998). *Class struggle: What's wrong (and right) with America's best public high schools.* New York, NY: Times Books.

Payne, R. K. (1998). *A framework for understanding poverty.* Baytown, TX: RFT.

Reeves, D. B. (2000). *Accountability in action: A blueprint for learning organizations.* Denver, CO: Advanced Learning Press.

Reeves, D. B. (2002). *The leader's guide to standards.* San Francisco, CA: Jossey-Bass.

Reeves, D. B. (2003). *Making standards work: How to implement standards-based assessments in the classroom, school, and district.* Denver, CO: Center for Performance Assessment.

Reeves, D. B. (2004a). *Accountability for learning.* Alexandria, VA: Association for Supervision and Curriculum Development.

Reeves, D. B. (2004b). *101 more questions and answers about standards, assessment, and accountability.* Englewood, CO: Advanced Learning Press.

Reeves, D. B. (2005). *101 questions & answers about standards, assessment, and accountability.* Englewood, CO: Advanced Learning Press.

Schmoker, M. (1996). *Results: The key to continuous school improvement.* Alexandria, VA: Association for Supervision and Curriculum Development.

Schmoker, M. (2006). *Results now, how we can achieve unprecedented improvements in teaching and learning.* Alexandria, VA: Association for Supervision and Curriculum Development.

Senge, P. M. (1990). *The fifth discipline: The art and practice of the learning organization.* New York, NY: Doubleday/Currency.

Tedlow, R. S. (2005, December 12). The education of Andy Grove. *Fortune, 152*(12). Retrieved from http://money.cnn.com/magazines/fortune/fortune_archive/2005/12/12/8363124/index.htm.

Westerberg, T. R. (2009). *Becoming a great high school—6 strategies and 1 attitude that make a difference.* Alexandria, VA: Association for Supervision and Curriculum Development.

Wiggins, G., & McTighe, J. (1998). *Understanding by design.* Alexandria, VA: Association for Supervision and Curriculum Development.

Index

Note: In page references, f indicates figures.

Academic achievement, 119–120
  See also Student performance
Accommodations, 122, 123
  legal mandates and, 119–120
  special education teachers and, 117–118
Accountability:
  discussion guide and, 37
  power standards and, 35
  quarterly instructional objectives
      and, 70, 71
  standards to power standards and, 157
  student learning and, 40
ACT, 79, 177
  understanding, 83
Administrators:
  curriculum and, 9, 13
  developing power standards and, 35
  keeping the project alive and, 134, 135
  power standards and, 54
  power standards feedback and, 48
  task force and, 23–24
  See also Staff members
Ainsworth, L., 12, 17, 41
Aligned assessments:
  developing, 79, 81, 82, 85, 91,
      102, 111, 112
  explanation of, 77–78
  plan/do/check/act cycle and, 79
  quarterly instructional objectives and,
      80–81, 92
  See also Assessments
Alignment, horizontal, 40, 41, 42, 68
Anxiety, student, 56
Articulation issues:
  power standards and, 41, 42, 44
  quarterly instructional objectives and, 64
Assessment companies, 87

Assessment documents:
  leadership issues and, 129
  project owner and, 32
  understanding, 33, 84
  See also Documents
Assessments:
  data and, 3
  deployment of, 106
  development of, 63–64, 81, 87–88
  development of local, 85, 89–90
  encore courses and, 85
  high-stakes, 36
  improving, 91–92
  learning and, 110
  legal mandates and, 119–120
  midterm/final, 80
  numbering system for, 105
  number of items on, 88
  political issues and, 111
  power standards and, 34
  publishing/storing, 105–106
  quarterly, 79
  quarterly feedback forms for, 100–101
  quarterly instructional objectives and,
      2–3, 59, 69, 70
  sample of, 102–104, 166–167
  scoring of, 108–109
  struggling students and, 80
  student progress and, 110
  student progress/power standards
      and, 36
  students with disabilities and, 116–119
  summative, 77–78
  understanding, 82–83
  See also Aligned assessments; Common
      assessments; Formative assessments;
      State assessments; Tests

Benchmarks:
    assessments and, 77
    discussion guide and, 37
    standards to power standards and, 157
Bloom's Taxonomy, 84
Boards of education:
    leadership issues and, 75
    power standards and, 57
Budgets, 22
    assessments and, 106
    groups and, 27, 29

Carter, L., 12, 84, 89
Change, xvi–xvii
    keeping the project alive and,
        133–136, 136
    local ownership/expertise and, 84
    mandatory assessments and, 106
    national standards and, 5
    power standards and, 53–54
    professional learning communities
        and, 22
    quarterly instructional objectives
        and, 71, 124
    staff development and, 120. *See also* Staff
        development
    systemic, 82, 137
    teachers and, 82
    time for, 111, 135
Coaching:
    staff development and, 120, 121.
        See also Staff development
Collaboration, 32
    special education teachers and, 117, 119
Common assessments, xv, xvi, xvii, xix, 2,
        18–19
    development of, 90–91
    keeping the project alive and, 135
    leadership issues and, 138
    power standards and, 40
    reasons for using, 78–81
    subskill scores and, 89
    See also Assessments
Communication issues:
    feedback and, 45, 133.
        See also Feedback
    groups and, 29
    keeping the project alive and, 135
    parents and, 55–56
    political issues and, 51
    power standards and, 39, 54–56
    quarterly instructional objectives
        and, 65, 71, 74

Consultants:
    legal mandates and, 120
    power standards and, 24
    staff development and, 121
    support and, 82
Continuous improvement issues, 19
    assessments and, 111–112
    developing/deploying power standards
        and, 51
    exceptional learners and, 124–125
    groups and, 29
    keeping the project alive and, 133
    quarterly instructional objectives and,
        65, 71, 73, 75
    success and, 82
Counselors, 32, 143
Curriculum, 7–10
    administrators and, 24
    aligned, 12f
    continual improvement of, 159
    disabilities and, 116–119
    discussions, 38
    districts and, 6, 10–11, 11f, 13
    documents, 14–15, 64
    encore courses and, 85
    groups and, 22–23
    improving, 91–92
    keeping the project alive and, 135, 136
    national models for, 9
    political issues and, 19
    power standards and, 18
    production issues and, 26
    quarterly instructional objectives
        and, 59, 81
    reform of, 71
    research and, 14–15
    special education teachers and, 117
    standardization of, 60–61
    state assessments and, 78
    state standards and, 8–9, 110
    students with disabilities and, 119
    yearly cycle and, 62
Curriculum alignment:
    group organization and, 25–26
    groups and, 22
    national standards and, 4, 5
    quarterly instructional objectives and, 63
    student performance and, 36
Curriculum-mapping, xxv

Data, 3
    assessments and, 79, 80
    decision-making and, 29

feedback and, 48, 101, 131, 132
instructional leadership talking points
    and, 49
keeping the project alive and, 133, 135–136
power standards and, 18
quarterly instructional objectives
    and, 64, 71
storing/using, 106–109
student performance and, 36, 73
walk-throughs and, 135–136
Decision-making:
    assessments and, 79
    feedback and, 128, 132
    groups and, 29
    outside consultants and, 24
    power standards and, 18
    quarterly instructional objectives and,
        61–62, 71
    real-time data and, 3
    state assessments and, 78
    teachers and, 13, 84
Department of Education, 24
Differentiated instruction, 121–122
Disabilities. *See* Students with disabilities
Discussion guides, 33–34
    quarterly instructional objectives
        and, 61
    standards to power standards, 37–38
District issues:
    accommodations and, 122
    curriculum and, 6, 10–11, 11f, 13
    curriculum/assessments and, 84
    development of common assessments
        and, 90–91
    final publication/use of power standards
        and, 50
    national standards and, 4–6
    noncore courses and, 85
    publishing power standards and, 55–56
    scoring and, 108–109. *See also* Scoring
    state standards/power standards
        and, 37–38
    students with disabilities and, 121
    support and, 82
    task force and, 22, 23–24
    understanding assessments and, 82–83
Diversity, 25, 143, 147
Do/check/act cycles:
    follow-up process guidelines for
        instructional objectives and, 159
    follow-up process guidelines for power
        standards and, 158
    power standards and, 41

Documents:
    curriculum, 14–15, 64
    curriculum/assessment, 129
    state, 32–33
    See also Assessment documents
Dolan, W. P., 132
Do What You Said You Would Do
    (DWYSYWD), 54, 107, 134
Dufour, R., 32

Edmonds, R., 137
Educational Service Center, 24
Educators:
    quarterly instructional objectives
        and, 71
    reforms and, 137
    understanding assessments and, 82–83
    See also Staff members
Encore courses, 85
English Curriculum Committee, 22–23
English language learners:
    differentiated instruction and, 121–122
    legal mandates and, 119–120
    mandatory learning and, 116
Environmental scan, 6
Exceptional education students. *See* English
    language learners

Faculty:
    designing power standards and, 22
    experimentation by, 81
    groups and, 87
    keeping the project alive and, 135
    meetings, 135
    quarterly instructional objectives and, 61
    See also Staff members
Feedback:
    continuous improvement issues and, 139
    dealing with, 131–133
    developing/deploying power standards
        and, 42, 51
    keeping the project alive and, 133, 135
    leadership issues and, 138
    power standards and, 42, 45–49
    quarterly instructional objectives
        and, 3, 61, 62, 69, 71, 72, 74
    success and, 127–128
Feedback forms, 130
    distributing, 132–133
    end-of-year, 164–165
    initial distribution of, 160–161
    keeping the project alive and, 133
    power standards and, 44, 45–47

quarterly assessments and,
100–102, 162–163
quarterly instructional objectives
and, 61, 73–74
Follow-up process guidelines, 44
power standards feedback and, 48
Formative assessments, 78
English language learner teachers
and, 118
strategies and, 122–123
See also Assessments
Freeport school district
plan-on-a-page, 142–145

Goals:
discussion guide and, 37
feedback and, 132
groups and, 26–28, 32, 50–51, 57–58
keeping the project alive and, 135
Grading issues, 78, 80, 106
See also Scoring
Groups:
assessments and, 80
collaboration and, 32
discussion guide and, 37
first draft of power standards and, 40–41
goals/roles/responsibilities of, 26–28, 32,
50–51, 57–58
membership and, 22–25
organization of, 25–26
power standards and, 39
purpose/commitment and, 22
quarterly instructional objectives and,
57–58, 63
rules and, 32
See also Professional learning
communities; Task force

High-stakes assessments, 36
See also Assessments
Horizontal alignment, 40, 41, 42, 68
Hunter, M., 51

Illinois Standards Achievement
Test (ISAT), 66, 142
Individuals with Disabilities Education
Act, 119
Instruction:
alignment of, 84
assessments and, 79
curriculum documents and, 14–15
differentiated, 121–122
improving, 109
keeping the project alive and, 135

reform of, 71
state assessments and, 78
Instructional focus calendars, 59–60
Instructional leadership talking points, 48, 49
Internet, 3
power standards and, 40
publishing power standards and, 55
See also Software

K–12:
publishing power standards and, 54–55
state standards and, 26
Kindergarten, 41, 71, 88, 153
state standards and, 26

Leadership issues, xvii, 4, 19, 137–138
administrators and, 9, 24
assessments and, 111
collaboration and, 118
curriculum and, 9
developing/deploying power standards
and, 51
differentiated instruction and, 122
exceptional learners and, 124
feedback and, 128, 129, 132, 138
groups and, 23, 25–26, 28
keeping the project alive and,
133, 134–135, 136
local educators and, 84
mandatory assessments and, 106
power standards and, 41, 54
power standards feedback and, 47–48
production issues and, 26
publishing power standards and, 55
quarterly instructional objectives
and, 74, 75
talking points and, 49
task force and, 22
time/structure for teachers and, 89
Learning. *See* Student learning
Learning communities. *See* Professional
learning communities
Legal issues:
differentiated instruction and, 122
mandates and, 116, 119–120
political issues and, 50, 139. *See also*
Political issues
power standards and, 57
Lesson plans, 2
keeping the project alive and, 135
quarterly instructional objectives
and, 64, 71
See also Planning
Lezotte, L., xviii, 5, 50, 78, 109, 116

Mandates, 116, 119–120
    staff development and, 120–121
Marzano, R. J., ix–x, 16
Math assessment, 166–167
McKee, K., xviii
McTighe, J., 3, 16
Modifications:
    definitions of, 122
    standardization of curriculum and, 117
Mundelein high school district, 146–147

NASSP, 16
National assessments:
    understanding, 82–83
    See also Assessments
National standards, 4–6
    state standards and, 18
    See also Standards
No Child Left Behind Act, 32
    discussion guide and, 37
    legal mandates and, 119–120
    power standards and, 35
    power standards feedback and, 45
    standards to power standards and, 157
Numbering systems:
    assessments and, 105
    quarterly instructional objectives and,
        65–69, 70, 88, 92

Observations:
    special education teachers and, 118
Outside consultants. See Consultants

Pacing guides, 2
    quarterly instructional objectives and,
        59–60
Parents:
    keeping the project alive and, 135
    publishing power standards and, 55–56
    quarterly instructional objectives
        and, 65, 69, 71
    understanding scoring and, 108
Partners4results software, xii, xxv, 3, 40
    assessments and, 69, 105
    identifying students with deficits in
        specific skills and, 92
    numbering system for assessments
        and, 105
    publishing power standards and, 54, 55
    quarterly instructional objectives
        and, 62, 64
    scoring and, 109
    storing assessments and, 106
    See also Software

Pepperi, C., 50
Performance goals, 119, 120
Plan, do, check, act cycle, xii, xix
    assessments and, 79, 80
    continuous improvement issues and,
        19, 112, 139
    curriculum alignment and, 3–4
    developing/deploying power standards
        and, 42, 51
    feedback and, 123, 128, 131, 132
    groups and, 28, 29
    keeping the project alive and, 135
    power standards and, 39
    publishing power standards and, 56
    quarterly instructional objectives and,
        58, 61, 62, 65, 71, 72, 75
    special education teachers and, 117
    staff development and, 120–121
    standardized curriculum and, 60–61
    validity/reliability and, 109
Planning:
    curriculum alignment and, 68
    English language learner teachers
        and, 118
    keeping the project alive and, 135
    leadership issues and, 75
    quarterly instructional objectives
        and, 64, 69, 70
    See also Lesson plans
Plan-on-a-page, x, xi, xxi, 142–145, 146–147
Political issues, xvii, 4
    assessments and, 80, 111
    curriculum and, 19
    developing/deploying power standards
        and, 50–51
    exceptional learners and, 124
    groups and, 28
    public education and, xix
    quarterly instructional objectives
        and, 74
Power standard 3M, 65–68, 69
Power standards, x–xi, xv–xvi, 12, 31,
    35–36
    assessments and, 79
    curriculum alignment and, 5
    defining, 16–18, 35–36
    deploying, 42–44, 54
    development of, 32, 35, 36,
        37–42, 61, 123
    discussion guide and, 37–38
    districts and, 22. See also District issues
    feedback forms for, 44, 45–48
    final publication/use of, 50
    first draft of, 40, 41

follow-up process guidelines for, 43, 158
gathering feedback and, 45–49
group organization and, 25–26
groups complete, 39
keeping the project alive and, 135, 136
leadership issues and, 138
local involvement and, 82
publication of, 44, 54–56
quarterly instructional objectives and,
    58–60. *See also* Quarterly
    instructional objectives
review of, 68
samples of, 149–155
selecting, 34
software and, 40. *See also* Software
staff development and, 120–121
standardized curriculum and, 60–61
standards and, 1–2, 34, 42, 157
technical issues and, xvi–xvii, 19
yearly review of, 73
Principals:
    feedback and, 47, 74, 131
    keeping the project alive and, 134, 136
    leadership issues and, 24
    publishing power standards and, 56
    See also Staff members
Process summary section, xviii–xix
Professional learning communities, 22
    assessments and, 80
    encore courses and, 85
    keeping the project alive and, 135
    mandates and, 116
    mandatory learning and, 116
    plan/do/check/act cycle and, 89
    special education teachers and, 118
    understanding assessments and, 83
    See also Groups
Professional learning teams, xi–xii
Project owners, 24
    collaboration and, 118
    group discussions and, 39
    groups and, 27
    power standards and, 39
    power standards feedback and, 48
    production issues and, 26
    publishing power standards and, 55
    state standard documents and, 32–33
    students with disabilities and, 116
    task force and, 28
Public education, 137–138
    quarterly instructional objectives and, 71
Publishing:
    assessments, 105–106
    power standards, 44, 54, 55–56, 56

quarterly instructional objectives,
    62, 70–74
tests, 105–106

Quarterly instructional objectives,
    xi, xv–xvi, 2, 51, 53
    assessments and, 79, 80–81
    defining, 58–60
    designing, 68
    development of, 32, 36, 61–65, 123
    final publication/use of power standards
        and, 50
    groups complete, 39
    keeping the project alive and, 135, 136
    leadership issues and, 138
    local involvement and, 82
    numbering system for, 65–69, 70, 88, 92
    power standards and, 40
    publishing/reviewing, 70–74
    realities of, 69–70
    review of, 68
    samples of, 102–104, 149–155
    special education teachers and, 117
    staff development and, 120–121
    standardized curriculum and, 60–61
    subskill scores and, 89
    teacher workload reduced by, 104–105, 118
    timeline and, 62
    yearly review of, 73
Questionnaire, 33, 34
Quizzes, 2–3
    See also Assessments; Tests

Rating scale, 130
Reading council, 23
Ready-made tests, 85–86
Reeves, D., 16, 18, 34, 78, 133
    contact information for, 169
Reflection, x, 4, 51, 120, 121
Reforms, 137–138
    quarterly instructional objectives and,
        71, 73
Regrouping strategies, 92
Response to intervention guidelines, 122–123
Response to intervention process, xvi, 110
Responsibilities:
    deploying power standards and, 42
    feedback and, 132
    groups and, 26–28, 32, 50–51, 57–58
    quarterly instructional objectives and, 71
Roles:
    feedback and, 132
    groups and, 26–28, 32, 50–51, 57–58
Rubrics, xii, 108, 110

School improvement plan, 134
School improvement team:
    feedback and, 131
    keeping the project alive and, 136
Schwartz, D., 22
Scoring, 80, 106
    assessments and, 108–109, 110
    rating scale and, 130
    state assessments and, 78
Skills:
    continuous improvement issues and, 19
    defining, 38
    discussion guide and, 37
    identifying students with deficits in
        specific, 92
    logical progression of, 68
    national standards and, 4
    power standards and, 39–40
    publishing power standards and, 44
    quarterly instructional objectives and,
        2, 58–59, 69, 70, 71
    selecting power standards and, 34
    special education teachers and, 117–118
    standards to power standards and, 157
    timeline and, 63
Software, xxv
    publishing power standards and, 55
    quarterly instructional objectives
        and, 62, 64, 71
    See also Partners4results software
Special education, 116
    legal mandates and, 119–120
    teachers, 117–118, 122, 124
    See also English language learners;
        Students with disabilities
Staff development, 21–22, 120–121
    assessments and, 80
    keeping the project alive and, 133
    legal mandates and, 120
    power standards feedback and, 45
Staff members:
    feedback and, 128, 129, 131, 133
    keeping the project alive and,
        133, 135, 136
    power standards and, 54
    superintendents, 24, 55
    training, 82–83
    See also Administrators; Educators;
        Faculty; Principals; Teachers
Standardized tests, 85–86
    See also Tests
Standards:
    assessments and, 80
    discussion guide and, 37–38

legal mandates and, 119–120
    most important, 38
    power standards and, 157
    students with disabilities and, 116–119
    unpacking, 36
    world-class, 4–5
    See also National standards; State
        standards
State assessment documents, 32–33
State assessments:
    curriculum alignment and, 36
    curriculum and, 11
    explanation of, 77–78
    local assessments and, 85
    quarterly instructional objectives and, 71
    secretive nature of, 13
    standards to power standards and, 157
    student performance and, 84
    understanding, 82–83
    See also Assessments; Tests
State standards:
    assessments and, 80
    complexity of, 35
    curriculum and, 7, 8–9, 110
    developing power standards and, 41
    group discussions about, 38–39
    local involvement and, 82
    national standards and, 4, 6
    power standards and, 1–2, 16–18, 34, 42
    production issues and, 26
    publishing power standards and, 44
    quarterly instructional objectives
        and, 58, 64, 71
    student performance and, 84
    See also Standards
Stiggins, R., 78, 79
    contact information for, 169
Student learning:
    accountability and, 40. See also
        Accountability
    assessments and, 78, 80, 110
    curriculum and, 81
    improving, 117
    mandatory, 116
    maximize, 68
    quarterly assessments and, 79
    quarterly instructional objectives and,
        59, 65, 69, 71, 74
    scoring and, 109
    selecting power standards and, 34
    state assessments and, 78
    teachers and, 105
    understanding state/national assessments
        and, 82–83

Student performance:
  assessments and, 79
  curriculum and, 14–15
  data and, 36
  improving, 137
  instruction/assessment/state standards
    and, 84
  keeping the project alive and,
    133, 135, 136
  quarterly instructional objectives
    and, 64, 71
  special education teachers and, 118
  standardized curriculum and, 60–61
  state summative assessments and, 78
Students:
  assessments and, 82–83
  identifying skill specific deficits and, 92
  instructional objective analysis of, 93–95f
  publishing power standards and, 56
  quarterly instructional objectives and,
    65, 69, 71
  skills and, 41. *See also* Skills
Students with disabilities:
  curriculum and, 116–119
  differentiated instruction and, 121–122
  legal mandates and, 119–120
  mandatory learning and, 116
  See also English language learners
Success:
  feedback and, 127–128
  groups and, 28
  local involvement and, 82
  quarterly instructional objectives and, 70
  selecting power standards and, 34
  students/assessments and, 84
  support and, 121
  total quality management/continuous
    improvement and, 82
Superintendents:
  project owners and, 24
  publishing power standards and, 55
  See also Staff members
Support:
  legal mandates and, 119–120
  staff development and, 121
Surveys:
  of current environment, 6–7
  curriculum reality and, 13
SWOT analysis, 6

Task force, 21–22, 32–33
  administrators and, 23–24
  deploying power standards and, 42–44

feedback and, 128, 131, 132
  feedback sheets and, 74
  groups and, 25–26, 29
  horizontal/vertical articulation and, 41, 44
  membership of, 22–23
  plan/do/check/act cycle and, 123–124
  power standards and, 31–32
  power standards feedback and, 45–48
  publishing power standards and, 44
  quarterly instructional objectives and,
    61, 63, 71, 74
  state standard documents and, 33
  understanding assessments and, 83
  See also Groups
Teacher contracts, 50–51
  assessments and, 111
  political issues and, 138
Teachers:
  assessments and, 80
  assessments mandatory for, 106
  change/support and, 82
  curriculum alignment and, 12
  curriculum and, 8–9, 10–11, 13
  decision-making and, 13, 84
  developing assessments and, 87–88
  developing power standards and, 35
  feedback and, 101, 129, 132
  formative assessments and, 78
  keeping the project alive and, 134–135, 136
  passionate about teaching, 37–38, 63
  power standards and, 32, 35, 54
  publishing power standards and, 55
  quarterly instructional objectives and,
    60, 64, 65, 69, 70, 71
  reducing workload for, 104–105, 118
  special education, 117–118, 122, 124.
    See also Special education
  state assessments and, 13, 34
  support and, 121
  task force and, 23–24
  understanding standards and, 17
  understanding state/national
    assessments and, 82–83
  See also Staff members
Teams:
  developing power standards and, 36
  professional learning, xi–xii
  school improvement, 131, 136
  special education teachers and, 117–118
Technical skills:
  assessments and, 112
  developing/deploying power standards
    and, 51

exceptional learners and, 125
    groups and, 29
    power standards and, xvi–xvii, 19
    quarterly instructional objectives and, 75
Test-prep materials, 86
Tests:
    ACT, 79, 83, 177
    power standards and, 35
    publishing/storing, 105–106
    purchasing, 85–86
    quarterly instructional objectives
        and, 2–3
    ready-made, 85–86
    state, 35. *See also* State assessments
    teacher-constructed, 86
    understanding, 82–83
    See also Assessments
Textbooks, 137
    end-of-chapter tests from, 86
    quarterly instructional objectives
        and, 63, 69
Time issues, 137
    change and, 111, 135
    curriculum alignment and, 134
    follow-up process guidelines for power
        standards and, 158
    local educators and, 84
    publishing power standards and, 44
    staff development and, 120, 121
    teachers and, 89

Total quality management, 3–4
    creation of, 32
    developing/deploying power standards
        and, 51
    groups and, 29
    keeping the project alive and, 133
    success and, 82
Turner, T., 137
Tutorials, 88

Unions, 111
    See also Teacher contracts

Walk-throughs, 135–136
Websites:
    accommodations and, 122
    differentiated instruction and, 121–122
    help at state, 83–84
    partners4results software and, 3, 40
    publishing power standards and, 55
    quarterly instructional objectives
        and, 59, 66
    software and, xxv
    state assessments and, 84
    storing assessments on, 106
    strategies and, 122
    students with disabilities and, 121
Westerberg, T. R., 16
Wiggins, G., 3, 16
World-class standards, 4–5

CORWIN

A SAGE Company

The Corwin logo—a raven striding across an open book—represents the union of courage and learning. Corwin is committed to improving education for all learners by publishing books and other professional development resources for those serving the field of PreK–12 education. By providing practical, hands-on materials, Corwin continues to carry out the promise of its motto: **"Helping Educators Do Their Work Better."**